WRITING GREEK

*An introduction to writing
in the language of Classical Athens*

Stephen Anderson
&
John Taylor

Bloomsbury Academic
An imprint of Bloomsbury Publishing Plc

B L O O M S B U R Y
LONDON · OXFORD · NEW YORK · NEW DELHI · SYDNEY

Bloomsbury Academic
An imprint of Bloomsbury Publishing Plc

50 Bedford Square	1385 Broadway
London	New York
WC1B 3DP	NY 10018
UK	USA

www.bloomsbury.com

**BLOOMSBURY and the Diana logo are trademarks of
Bloomsbury Publishing Plc**

First published by Bristol Classical Press 2010
Reprinted by Bloomsbury Academic 2014, 2015

British Library Cataloguing-in-Publication Data
A catalogue record for this book is available from the British Library.

ISBN: PB: 978-1-8539-9717-4
ePDF: 978-1-4725-0285-8
ePUB: 978-1-4725-0286-5

Library of Congress Cataloging-in-Publication Data
A catalog record for this book is available from the Library of Congress.

Typeset by John Taylor

Contents

Introduction   vii
List of abbreviations   ix
Glossary of grammar terms   x

PART 1

Chapter 1   Basic use of cases   1
Chapter 2   Definite article   6
Chapter 3   Time, place and space   10
Chapter 4   Use of adjectives   15
Chapter 5   Verb tenses   19
Chapter 6   Participles I   22
Chapter 7   Pronouns I   25
Chapter 8   Pronouns II   30
Chapter 9   Relative clauses   35
Chapter 10   Connection   38

PART 2

Chapter 11   Indirect statement   41
Chapter 12   Questions   48
Chapter 13   Commands, exhortations and wishes   55
Chapter 14   Purpose clauses   61
Chapter 15   Result clauses   66
Chapter 16   Conditional sentences   71
Chapter 17   Participles II   79
Chapter 18   Verbs of fearing, precaution and
             preventing   85
Chapter 19   Indefinites   91
Chapter 20   Temporal clauses   94
Chapter 21   Impersonal verbs; Accusative absolute;
             Gerundives   100

Appendices

1	Passages from North and Hillard	107
2	Uses of the subjunctive and optative	113
3	Negatives and their main uses	114
4	Prepositions	117
5	Accents	122
6	Principal parts of 100 important irregular verbs	128

Vocabulary 140

Index 174

Introduction

Fewer people nowadays than ever before learn how to write in Classical
Greek. In no public or university degree examination is composition
compulsory, and there is no shortage of scholars and teachers ready at the
drop of a hat to pour scorn on the whole business.

Why, then, a new Greek composition textbook? Aren't the 'old faithfuls' of
the last century, and the one before, perfectly adequate for those who wish to
engage in this curious, antiquarian pursuit?

In writing this brand new book we wish to encourage as many Greek
students as possible, in both schools and universities, to have a go at prose
composition. A traditional exercise it may well be, but it is far from a
valueless one: not only does it provide an excellent means of learning the
language's grammatical 'nuts and bolts', but also, the very attempt to
produce accurate and elegant prose helps students understand the challenges
faced by the ancient writers themselves, and enables them to appreciate
better their achievement in the texts which survive.

The book is divided into two parts. Part 1 deals mainly with the component
elements of the simple sentence, whilst in Part 2 all major constructions are
covered. Each chapter contains a fuller grammatical explanation than will be
found in older textbooks, followed by two or three exercises of practice
sentences, and further supplemented, from Chapter 10 on, by passages for
continuous composition. These passages are as a rule a little longer than in
many composition books, sometimes even running to two paragraphs.
Teachers can treat them as they choose, and may like to consider the
possibility of doing some of a passage together in class, leaving the rest to be
done by students on their own. There is, too, a series of helpful appendices,
including one containing a selection from the best of North and Hillard's
passages, and finishing with a list of 100 irregular verbs and a
comprehensive vocabulary.

John Taylor wrote Part 1 of the book, and supplied Appendices 4, 5 and 6.
He wishes to thank Stephen Anderson for many helpful comments and
corrections.

Stephen Anderson wrote Part 2, Appendices 1, 2 and 3, and the vocabulary. He did most of the work whilst on sabbatical during the Michaelmas Term of 2009 and the Lent Term of 2010. He would like to thank the Headmaster of Winchester for granting the leave, and the Master and Fellows of St. John's College, Cambridge for taking him in and providing not only the ideal surroundings for such a project, but also students on whom to test the exercises.

Further and in particular, he would like to thank two old friends, James Morwood and Ian McAuslan, for reading all his work in draft, correcting his mistakes and making many helpful suggestions for improvement.

We should both like to thank Ray Davies, Deborah Blake and all at Duckworth for having such confidence in us and for seeing us through to publication.

Stephen Anderson   John Taylor
Winchester College   Tonbridge School

Abbreviations

abl.	ablative
abs.	absolute
acc.	accusative
act.	active
adj.	adjective
adv.	adverb
aor.	aorist
conj.	conjunction
dat.	dative
f.	feminine
gen.	genitive
impers.	impersonal
impf.	imperfect
infin.	infinitive
intrans.	intransitive
lit.	literally
m.	masculine
n.	neuter
nom.	nominative
pass.	passive
pf.	perfect
pl.	plural
prep.	preposition
pres.	present
rel.	relative
sc.	(Latin *scilicet*) understand, supply (word/s not actually given)
sing.	singular
trans.	transitive
voc.	vocative

Glossary of grammar terms

absolute	grammatically unconnected with the rest of the sentence (literally *separated off*), as in *genitive absolute* and *accusative absolute*.
accidence	the part of grammar that deals with word endings (as distinct from *syntax*).
accusative	case of direct object; used with some prepositions, usually expressing *motion towards*; used to express *time how long*; used for subject of infinitive or participle in indirect statement and other constructions, if different from subject of main verb; the (neuter) participle of an impersonal verb unconnected with the rest of its sentence is an *accusative absolute*.
active	form of verb where the grammatical subject is the doer of the action (one of three *voices,* as distinct from *middle* or *passive*).
adjective	word describing a noun (with which it *agrees* in number, gender and case).
adverb	word describing a verb (or an adjective, or another adverb).
agent	person by whom an action is done, usually expressed by ὑπό with genitive after a passive verb (but dative alone always after verbal adjective/gerundive, and optionally after perfect/pluperfect passive).
agree	have the same number (agreement of subject and verb); have the same number, gender and case (agreement of noun and adjective).
ambiguous	can mean more than one thing.
antecedent	person or thing in main clause to which relative pronoun (or adverb) refers back.
aorist	tense of a verb referring to a single action in the past (as distinct from *imperfect, perfect* and *pluperfect*); in all uses of the aorist imperative and subjunctive, most uses of the aorist infinitive and optative, and some uses of the aorist participle, the aorist is used by *aspect* (rather than tense) to express simply a single action, not necessarily in the past.
apodosis	the main clause of a conditional sentence, expressing the

	consequence (i.e. not the *if* half, which is the *protasis*).
apposition	use of a word or phrase parallel in grammar to another, to give more information (e.g. *Sophocles, the poet, ...* : two nouns *in apposition*).
article	(see *definite article*).
aspect	the expression of *type of time* (single or repeated/ extended action), as distinct from actual time (past, present, future) which is *tense*.
attraction	in a relative clause, the process by which a genitive or dative antecedent makes a relative pronoun agree with it (overriding the normal rule that its case is determined by its job within the relative clause).
augment	epsilon put on the front of a verb to denote a past tense.
auxiliary	a verb (usually part of *to be*) used with a participle to form a tense of another verb.
breathing	symbol above a vowel or diphthong (or rho) beginning a word, indicating presence (*rough* breathing: ἁ- = *ha*) or absence (*smooth* breathing: ἀ- = *a*) of *h* sound or *aspiration*. Either breathing comes on the *second* vowel of a diphthong (αὐ-, αὑ-).
cardinal	ordinary numeral (1, 2, 3), as distinct from *ordinal* (first, second, third).
case	form of a noun, pronoun or adjective that shows the job it does in the sentence (e.g. accusative for direct object); cases are arranged in the order nominative, (vocative), accusative, genitive, dative.
clause	part of a sentence with its own subject and verb.
common	(referring to gender): can be either masculine or feminine according to context (e.g. ὁ/ἡ παῖς *boy/girl*).
comparative	form of an adjective or adverb meaning *more, -er*.
complement	another nominative word or phrase describing the subject.
compound	verb with prefix (e.g. ἀποβάλλω *I throw away*); adjective or negative made up of more than one element.
concessive	expressing the idea *although* or *despite* (expressed by καίπερ with participle).
conditional	expressing *if* or *unless* (the clause beginning *if* or *unless* is the *protasis*, the other half - expressing the result - is the *apodosis*).
conjugate	go through in order the different parts of a verb: first,

	second, third person singular, then plural (as distinct from *decline*, used for a noun, pronoun, adjective or participle).
conjunction	word joining clauses, phrases or words together (e.g. *and, but, therefore*).
consonant	letter representing a sound that can only be used together with a vowel.
construction	pattern according to which a particular type of sentence or clause (e.g. indirect statement) is formed.
correlatives	set of linked interrogative/indefinite/relative/ demonstrative adverbs or pronouns (e.g. *where?/ somewhere/[the place]where/there*).
contraction	process by which two adjacent vowels (or vowel plus diphthong) coalesce into a single vowel or diphthong.
crasis	process by which a vowel or diphthong at the end of a word coalesces with another at the start of the next word, the result written as a single word instead of two separate ones (e.g. ὦνδρες for ὦ ἄνδρες).
dative	case of indirect object, often translated *to* or *for*; used with prepositions, often to express *position* or *rest* (as distinct from motion); used to express *time when*.
declension	one of the patterns (three main ones, also used for pronouns, adjectives and participles) by which nouns change their endings.
decline	go through a noun, pronoun, adjective or participle in case order, singular then plural (as distinct from *conjugate*, used of tenses of a verb).
definite article	ὁ ἡ τό (equivalent to English *the*, but used more widely).
deliberative	use of the subjunctive to express a thought process (e.g. *should I do X?*).
demonstrative	pronoun, adjective or adverb pointing out some feature of a situation (e.g. *this, that, there, then*).
deponent	verb which has only middle (or sometimes passive) forms, but is active in meaning.
diphthong	two consecutive vowels pronounced as one syllable (e.g. αυ, ει, ευ).
direct object	noun or pronoun on receiving end of the action of verb.
direct speech	actual words of a speaker, usually signalled by initial capital letter or enclosed by inverted commas.
dual	special set of endings expressing two items, or two

	subjects of a verb (relic of an earlier stage of the language when plural implied three or more).
elision	dropping of a (usually short) vowel at the end of a word before another beginning with a vowel, indicated by an apostrophe (e.g. τ' for τε).
enclitic	literally *leaning on*: a (usually short and unaccented) word which cannot stand alone but must follow another word (e.g. the indefinite τις).
ending	last bit of a word, added to the stem to give more detail and show its job.
feminine	one of the three genders, for females or things imagined as female.
finite	form of a verb with tense and person ending (as distinct from infinitive or participle).
future	tense of verb referring to something that will happen in the future.
gender	one of three categories (masculine, feminine, neuter) into which nouns and pronouns are put according to their actual or imagined sex or lack of it.
genitive	case expressing possession or definition, often translated *of*; used in expressions indicating e.g. *part of, some of*; used with some prepositions, usually expressing *motion away from*; used after a comparative to mean *than*; used to express *time within which*; noun and participle phrase grammatically unconnected with the rest of its sentence is a *genitive absolute*; follows some verbs expressing ideas such as *take hold of*.
gerund	a verb made into a noun (*the act of doing X*), expressed by τό with infinitive.
gerundive	adjective formed from verb, expressing the idea *needing to be done*.
historic	set of tenses (imperfect, aorist, pluperfect) referring to the past (as distinct from *primary* ones referring to the present or future), and determining the *sequence* according to which subordinate clauses are constructed (e.g. use of optative rather than subjunctive); *historic present* is the use of the present tense for a story set in the past (to achieve vividness).
homonym	word coincidentally spelled in the same way as another unconnected word.

idiom	distinctive form of expression within a language, established by common use but going beyond what can be worked out from the individual words.
imperative	form of verb used for direct command.
imperfect	tense of verb referring to incomplete, extended or repeated action in the past.
impersonal	third person singular verb whose subject is *it*.
indeclinable	does not change its endings.
indefinite	(1) *indefinite article*: the English *a(n)*, which has no direct equivalent in Greek, though the indefinite τις (*someone/a certain*) can be used. (2) *indefinite adverb* or *pronoun* (in a set of correlatives): often the same in form as the equivalent indirect interrogative word, but with no accent or different accent; the indefinite relative is ὅστις (*anyone who*). (3) *indefinite construction*: clause expressing an unspecific *whoever, whenever* etc, expressed in Greek by ἄν with subjunctive in primary sequence, and by optative alone in historic sequence.
indicative	form of verb expressing a fact (as distinct from other *moods* expressing e.g. possibilities).
indirect	indirect statement, command or question is the reported form of it (as distinct from quotation of the speaker's actual words); indirect object is person or thing in the dative indirectly affected by object of verb, e.g. *I gave the money* (direct object) *to the old man* (indirect object).
infinitive	form of verb introduced by *to*, expressing the basic meaning (e.g. παύειν *to stop*). Greek verbs have several infinitives to express differences of tense and voice (e.g. future passive infinitive παυσθήσεσθαι *to be going to be stopped*).
inflection	technical term for *ending*: as an inflected language, Greek depends heavily on word endings to express meaning.
intransitive	verb that does not have a direct object (e.g. βαίνω *I go*).
irregular	word that does not follow one of the standard patterns of declension or conjugation.
main clause	clause which can stand alone, and expresses the main point of a sentence (as distinct from *subordinate* clause).

masculine | one of the three genders, for males or things imagined as male.

middle | form of a verb expressing a relation of subject to action which is thought of as midway between active and passive, but is often actually both (e.g. reflexive *I wash myself* or causative *I get something washed*); *deponent* verbs have middle/passive forms, but often with simply active meaning.

mood | set of forms of a verb showing whether it is indicative, imperative, subjunctive or optative.

negative | expressing that something is not the case or should not happen.

neuter | one of the three genders, for things imagined as neither male nor female.

nominative | case used for subject of sentence, or of any finite verb, or of infinitive or participle (in indirect statement and other constructions) if the same as the subject of the main verb.

noun | word naming a person or thing (e.g. πόλις *city*); a *proper* noun with a capital letter gives its actual name (e.g. Ἀθῆναι *Athens*).

number | being either singular or plural (or sometimes dual).

numerals | numbers, either *cardinal* (one, two, three) or *ordinal* (first, second, third).

object | noun or pronoun acted upon by a verb.

optative | form of verb (often expressed in English by *might*) expressing a wish or a not very likely possibility (as distinct from the indicative for a fact, and the subjunctive for a more likely possibility); in many constructions the subjunctive is used in *primary sequence*, the optative in *historic sequence*.

ordinal | type of numeral expressing order (first, second, third), as an adjective, as distinct from *cardinal* (1, 2, 3).

part of speech | category of word (noun, adjective, pronoun, verb, adverb, preposition, conjunction).

particle | short indeclinable word (often conjunction or adverb) connecting things together, or giving emphasis or colour (e.g. οὖν *therefore*; δή *indeed*).

participle | adjective formed from a verb (e.g. παύων *stopping*).

partitive | use of the genitive to express *part of, some of* etc.

passive | form of verb where the subject does not do the action but

xv

	is on the receiving end of it (e.g. παύομαι *I am stopped*).
perfect	tense of verb referring to a completed action in the past, whose effects still continue (e.g. *our friends have arrived*); in Greek a *primary* tense, often virtually equivalent to present. (A single action in the past is expressed by the much more common *aorist*.)
person	term for the subject of verb: first person *I, we*; second person *you* (singular or plural); third person *he, she, it, they* (or a noun replacing one of these).
phrase	group of words not containing a finite verb (as distinct from *clause*).
pluperfect	tense of verb referring to something that had already happened by a particular point in the past, and whose effects were continuing when something else happened.
plural	more than one (as distinct from singular, or sometimes from dual).
positive	not negative; (of adjectives) the ordinary form, indicating simply that the person or thing has the quality described (as distinct from *comparative* and *superlative*, expressing the degree to which they have it).
possessive	adjective or pronoun expressing who or what something belongs to; *possessive dative* is the idiom e.g. *there is to me a dog* for *I have a dog*.
potential	something that *might* happen (often expressed by ἄν and the optative).
prefix	word or syllable added to the beginning of another word.
preposition	word used with a noun or pronoun in the accusative, genitive or dative to focus more closely the meaning of the case (e.g. *into, away from, on*).
present	tense of a verb referring to something that is happening now, or of a participle referring to something happening at the same time as the main verb.
primary	set of tenses (present, future, perfect) referring to the present or future (as distinct from *historic* ones referring to the past), and determining the *sequence* according to which subordinate clauses are constructed (e.g. use of subjunctive rather than optative).
principal parts	first person singulars of important tenses of a verb, from which other forms and necessary information about it can be worked out.

prohibition	negative command (*don't do X!*), expressed by μή with present imperative for a general prohibition, or μή with aorist subjunctive for one occasion.
pronoun	word that stands instead of a noun, avoiding the need to repeat it.
protasis	the *if...* half of a conditional sentence (in negative form *if... not* or *unless* ...).
reduplication	process by which the initial consonant of a verb is added again on the front followed by epsilon, to make the perfect tense (e.g. παύω, perfect πέπαυκα).
reflexive	word referring back to the subject of the verb.
regular	a word which forms its endings according to a standard pattern.
relative	subordinate clause (or pronoun/adverb introducing it) relating to person or thing just mentioned in the main clause (who or which is the *antecedent*).
root	basic stem of verb, or element from which a group of related words are derived.
sentence	group of words with subject and verb (and often other elements), which can stand on its own (as distinct from *phrase* or *subordinate clause*).
sequence	process by which the tense of the main clause determines the construction of a subordinate clause (e.g. whether its verb is subjunctive or optative).
singular	just one (as distinct from dual or plural).
stem	the part of a word which stays the same: different endings are added to show the job it does in the sentence.
subject	noun or pronoun in the nominative case, expressing who or what does the action (with active verb) or is on the receiving end of it (with passive verb).
subjunctive	form of verb (often expressed in English by *may*) referring to an idea or possibility (as distinct from *indicative* for a fact, or *optative* for a more remote possibility); in some constructions the subjunctive is used in *primary sequence*, the optative in *historic sequence*.
subordinate	of secondary importance to something else; a subordinate clause cannot stand alone but only makes sense in relation to the main clause.
suffix	word or syllable added to the end of another word.
superlative	form of adjective/adverb meaning *very, (the) most, -est*.

syllable	part of a word forming a spoken unit, usually consisting of vowel with consonants before or after or both.
syntax	the part of grammar that deals with sentences and constructions (as distinct from *accidence*).
tense	form of a verb showing when the action takes place (in the past, present or future).
transitive	verb that has a direct object.
understand	provide in translation a word which is not separately represented in Greek but must be worked out from the grammar and context (e.g. *men* or *things* from the gender of an adjective or part of the definite article).
verb	word expressing an action.
vividness	principle by which past events, words or thoughts are envisaged as present (to give a sense of immediacy), so that a primary construction is used rather than the historic one strictly required (e.g. indicative in indirect statement/ question, or subjunctive in purpose clause, rather than optative).
vocative	case used for addressing someone or something.
voice	one of three sets of verb forms (active, middle, passive) showing how the subject relates to the action.
vowel	letter representing a sound that can be spoken by itself: α, ε, η, ι, ο, υ, ω.

PART 1

Chapter 1: Basic use of cases

Nominative

The *nominative* case is used for the subject of a finite verb (i.e. one with a tense and person ending), in a main or subordinate clause.

> *The Athenians fled.*
> οἱ Ἀθηναῖοι ἔφυγον.

> *When the Athenians had fled, the people on the island rejoiced.*
> ἐπεὶ οἱ Ἀθηναῖοι ἔφυγον, οἱ ἐν τῇ νήσῳ ἐχάρησαν.

• Another noun in apposition to the subject is also nominative.

> *Socrates, a wise man, said these things.*
> ὁ Σωκράτης, ἀνὴρ σοφός, εἶπε ταῦτα.

• Likewise the nominative is used for the complement of verbs such as *be* and *become*.

> *Xenophon then became leader.*
> ὁ Ξενοφῶν τότε ἡγεμὼν ἐγένετο.

The noun which is the complement normally does not have the definite article.

Vocative

The *vocative* case is used for direct address, with or without ὦ (*O* ...):

> *The enemy are attacking us, citizens!*
> οἱ πολέμιοι προσβάλλουσιν ἡμῖν, ὦ πολῖται.

1

The vocative often occurs with the imperative (see Chapter 13).

> *Listen, citizens!*
> ἀκούσατε, ὦ πολῖται.

Accusative

The *accusative* case is used for the direct object of a verb.

> *The girl chased the dog.*
> ἡ παῖς ἐδίωξε τὸν κύνα.

Some verbs (e.g. *teach*, *ask*) take a double accusative (e.g. *she taught me Greek*; contrast *he gave me food*, where *me* is a dative indirect object).

Non-finite parts of the verb (infinitive and participle) can take an object.

• The accusative is used with many prepositions, especially those expressing *motion towards*.

> *The boy ran towards the field.*
> ὁ παῖς πρὸς τὸν ἀγρὸν ἔδραμεν.

• The accusative is used to specify the *part affected* (sometimes called *accusative of respect*).

> *The soldier was wounded in the foot.*
> ὁ στρατιώτης ἐτραυματίσθη τὸν πόδα.

Genitive

The *genitive* case is used to express possession, and other meanings corresponding to English *of*.

I admire the wisdom of the old man (the old man's wisdom).
θαυμάζω τὴν τοῦ γέροντος σοφίαν.

Note here the *genitive sandwich* (the genitive article + noun specifying the possessor goes inside the article + noun specifying the thing possessed, hence two parts of the article occur in succession).

• The genitive is used to express the group or larger entity of which something is a part (*partitive* gentive).

> *Many of the slaves are working.*
> πολλοὶ τῶν δούλων ἐργάζονται.

As an extension of this, the genitive is used after verbs expressing ideas such as *get hold of.*
> *The man got hold of the boy's arm.*
> ὁ ἀνὴρ ἐλάβετο τῆς τοῦ παιδὸς χειρός.

The verb ἀκούω (*I hear*) normally takes the genitive of a person, accusative of a thing.

• The genitive is used with some prepositions, especially those expressing *motion away from.*

> *The children are running away from the danger.*
> οἱ παῖδες ἀπὸ τοῦ κινδύνου τρέχουσιν.

• The genitive is used with the preposition ὑπό (*by*) for the agent of a passive verb (the person by whom the action is done).

> *The book was written by the woman.*
> ἡ βίβλος ἐγράφη ὑπὸ τῆς γυναικός.

Dative

The *dative* case is used to express the indirect object of the verb (in English often translated *to* or *for*).

> *The woman gave the food to the old man (gave the old man the food).*
> ἡ γυνὴ ἔδωκε τὸν σῖτον τῷ γέροντι.

In English *to* is normally missed out if the indirect object precedes the direct.

As an extension of this, the dative is used after verbs like *trust* and *obey* (give trust/obedience *to* someone).
> *The doctor trusted the letter.*
> ὁ ἰατρὸς ἐπίστευσε τῇ ἐπιστολῇ.

• The dative is used with some prepositions, especially those expressing *rest in* a place.

> *The friends were waiting in the forest.*
> οἱ φίλοι ἐν τῇ ὕλῃ ἔμενον.

• The dative is used for the *instrument* of a passive verb (the thing with which the action is done).

> *The boy was hit with a stone.*
> ὁ παῖς λίθῳ ἐβλήθη.

The dative can be used (instead of ὑπό and the genitive) for the agent with the perfect or pluperfect passive.

• The *possessive* dative expresses who something belongs to.

> *I have a dog (*literally *there is to me a dog).*
> ἔστι μοι κύων.

This is a common alternative to κύνα ἔχω (*I have a dog*).

Exercises

A

1   The children were walking towards the sea.
2   The queen, a wise woman, found out the truth.
3   A few of the slaves are still here.
4   The sailor's brother was made leader of the citizens.
5   The judge's friends will soon arrive.
6   The soldier was wounded in the head with a sword.
7   The woman returned from the market-place to the house.
8   The book was seen by the teacher.
9   I will give the girl a gift.
10 The boy has a beautiful dog.

B

1   The judge taught his son the words.
2   Many of the women admired the doctor.
3   It is necessary to be silent, old man, in the general's house.
4   The girls lived in the village with the teacher's wife.
5   I have a new horse.
6   We shall soon hear the voice of the god.
7   The prisoner saw a ship in the harbour.
8   I do not trust the politician's words.
9   The dog got hold of the woman's foot.
10 The slave escaped out of the house.

Chapter 2: Definite article

The *definite article* (ὁ ἡ τό) is used in virtually all situations where English uses *the*, and in some others. Essentially it indicates definiteness or specifies a *particular one*.

An exception is the frequent use of βασιλεύς alone (without article or any other specification) for the uniquely important king of Persia.

Greek has no indefinite article *a* (pl. *some*) - hence just δοῦλοι for *some slaves* - but can use the indefinite τις (*a certain*) to be a bit more specific (see Chapter 8).

1   With a noun, like English *the*. Also for general classes, and abstractions.

> *poets* (in general)   *time*
> οἱ ποιηταί   ὁ χρόνος

• Often but not always used with proper names, especially if well-known, or already mentioned.

> *Greece*   *Zeus*
> ἡ Ἑλλάς   ὁ Ζεύς

When translating sentences into Greek, putting the article with a proper name is never wrong.

2   With an adjective, to make a noun.

> *the free, free men*   *(the) truth*
> οἱ ἐλεύθεροι   τὸ ἀληθές

3   With an adverb, to make a noun.

> *men/people of old*   *women now, women of today*
> οἱ πάλαι   αἱ νῦν

4   With a preposition phrase, to make a noun.

the people on the island   (the) affairs in the city
οἱ ἐν τῇ νήσῳ   τὰ ἐν τῇ πόλει

All these examples (2, 3 and 4) are essentially incomplete sandwiches: hence οἱ νῦν δοῦλοι would be *present-day slaves*.

5   With an infinitive, to make a verbal noun (the *articular infinitive*, equivalent to the gerund in Latin).

(the act of) running
τὸ τρέχειν

The infinitive is here treated as a neuter noun; it cannot itself decline, but the accompanying article can.
  the art of writing
  ἡ τοῦ γράφειν τέχνη

An adverb can be inserted.
  by speaking well
  τῷ εὖ λέγειν

The negative in this idiom is μή.
  by not looking
  τῷ μὴ βλέπειν

If a subject is expressed (between the article and the infinitive), it is nominative if the same as the subject of the sentence, accusative if different.
  I am not surprised at the fact that human beings make mistakes.
  οὐ θαυμάζω τὸ τοὺς ἀνθρώπους ἁμαρτάνειν.

The translation e.g. *running* for this idiom must be distinguished from the present active participle (*while running*): see Chapter 6 for this, and for the use of the article with a participle (e.g. οἱ τρέχοντες *those running/those who run/[the] runners*).

6   Sandwiching possessive genitive (see Chapter 1), adjective (see Chapter 4), adverb or preposition phrase.

the doctor's house   *the wise old man*
ἡ τοῦ ἰατροῦ οἰκία   ὁ σοφὸς γέρων

7   Repeated, with the same effect as a sandwich.

the doctor's house   *the wise old man*
ἡ οἰκία ἡ τοῦ ἰατροῦ   ὁ γέρων ὁ σοφός

This (rather than sandwiching) is the norm when a participle is attached to a noun to specify which one (see Chapter 6).
    the fleeing slave
    ὁ δοῦλος ὁ φεύγων

8   With μέν ... δέ (see Chapter 10) to contrast individuals or groups (often found with a partitive genitive).

One man was killed, the other was wounded.
ὁ μὲν ἀπέθανεν, ὁ δὲ ἐτραυματίσθη.

Some of the slaves stayed, others fled.
οἱ μὲν τῶν δούλων ἔμειναν, οἱ δὲ ἔφυγον.

This idiom is a fossilised survival of the use in pre-classical Greek of the article as a pronoun.

9   With δέ, changing the subject to someone who was mentioned in the previous sentence or clause but was not its subject.

I called the slave - but he did not hear.
ἐκάλεσα τὸν δοῦλον· ὁ δὲ οὐκ ἤκουσεν.

In this idiom context determines whether *and* or *but* is more natural in English. Like 8 above, it is a survival of the older use of the article as a pronoun.

Exercises

A

1   The people in the market-place are strangers.
2   Fighting does not always bring victory.
3   The girls are learning the art of writing well.
4   I sent for the slave - and he soon arrived.
5   The people there admire the doctor's house.
6   The mountain on the island is not high.
7   Poets teach many things.
8   The men in the assembly were listening to the messenger.
9   Affairs in the city were then bad.
10 The politician was being praised on account of speaking well.

B

1   The people on the ship heard a strange voice.
2   The king of Persia's messenger arrived yesterday.
3   Some of the boys went away, others are still here.
4   Time brings wisdom.
5   The woman in the street heard the shout.
6   The gods were often guests of the men of old.
7   One woman fled, the other stayed.
8   By not despairing we finally saved the city.
9   Beauty is worth much.
10 The women in the village prepared a big dinner.

Chapter 3: Time, place and space

Time

- The <u>accusative</u> is used to express *time how long*.

> *The girl's father was away for two months.*
> ὁ τῆς παιδὸς πατὴρ δύο μῆνας ἀπῆν.

> *The treaty lasted for three years.*
> αἱ σπονδαὶ τρία ἔτη ἔμενον.

- The <u>genitive</u> is used to express *time within which*.

> *The allies will arrive within four days.*
> οἱ σύμμαχοι τεσσάρων ἡμερῶν ἀφίξονται.

> *The woman fell ill during the night.*
> ἡ γυνὴ τῆς νυκτὸς ἐνόσησεν.

- The <u>dative</u> is used to express *time when*.

> *On the fifth day we saw a ship.*
> τῇ πέμπτῃ ἡμέρᾳ εἴδομεν ναῦν.

> *The girls returned the next day.*
> αἱ παῖδες τῇ ὑστεραίᾳ ἐπανῆλθον.

In all these examples, note that words such as *for*, *within*, *during*, *on* are not separately translated by prepositions but simply represented by using the appropriate case. An exception to this is that ἐν (*in*) is quite often found with the dative, e.g. ἐν τῷ χειμῶνι (*in winter*), where the meaning hovers between time within which and time when.

Note that the accusative and genitive versions naturally use cardinal numbers, the dative version ordinal ones. These may be contrasted in the same sentence.

We were marching for four days; on the fifth we finally arrived.
τέσσαρας μὲν ἡμέρας ἐπορευόμεθα, τῇ δὲ πέμπτῃ τέλος ἀφικόμεθα.

• More specialised expressions of time commonly use prepositions. Note the following:

ἅμ᾽ ἡμέρᾳ	at daybreak
δι᾽ ὀλίγου	after a short time, soon
διὰ πέντε ἐτῶν	every five years
εἰς καιρόν	at the right time
ἐκ τούτου	after this, as a result of this
ἐν τούτῳ	meanwhile (*sc.* τῷ χρόνῳ)
ἐν ᾧ	while (*sc.* χρόνῳ)
καθ᾽ ἡμέραν	daily, every day
μετὰ ταῦτα	after this
πρὸς ἑσπέραν	towards evening
τῇ προτεραίᾳ	on the previous day
τῇ ὑστεραίᾳ	on the next day
τοῦ λοιποῦ	in the future (*sc.* χρόνου)
ὑπὸ νύκτα	just before nightfall

Place

Place is usually expressed by a preposition followed by the appropriate case (see Appendix 4).

• Prepositions with the <u>accusative</u> are used for *motion towards* or the idea of *traversing*:

εἰς τὴν πόλιν	into the city
ἀνὰ τὸ ὄρος	up the mountain
παρὰ τὸν ποταμόν	along the river
πρὸς τὸν ἀγρόν	towards the field
παρὰ τὸν βασιλέα	to/into the presence of the king
ὡς τὸν ἰατρόν	to the doctor

Note that ὡς or παρά rather than πρός is normally used for motion towards a *person*.

• Prepositions with the <u>genitive</u> are used for *motion away from*:

ἀπὸ τοῦ λιμένος	away from the harbour
ἐκ τῆς οἰκίας	out of the house
κατὰ τοῦ ὄρους	down from the mountain
παρὰ τοῦ βασιλέως	from the king

Note that παρὰ rather than ἀπό is normally used for motion away from a *person*.

• Prepositions with the <u>dative</u> are used for *place where* or *rest in* a place:

ἐν τῇ κώμῃ	in the village
παρ' ἡμῖν	at our place/house (*like Latin* apud *or French* chez)
πρὸς τῇ θαλάσσῃ	near the sea

Note that place names in the dative can be used with or without ἐν.

Note that many prepositions can take more than one case. Prepositions focus a meaning which the case has already. Thus for example παρά basically means *beside*: hence with the accusative the underlying idea is *to/along beside*, with the genitive *from beside*, and with the dative *resting beside*.

There are however some exceptions, e.g. ἐφ' ἵππου (*on horseback*) which uses the genitive where the dative might have been expected.

• There are a few examples of a special locative case expressing *place where*:

Ἀθήνησι(ν)	in Athens
οἴκοι	at home
χαμαί	on the ground

Some words have the suffix -δε or -σε to indicate *place to where*:

Ἀθήναζε	to Athens (= Ἀθήνας + δε)
οἴκαδε	(to) home, homewards
πανταχόσε	in all directions

Some words have the suffix -θεν to indicate *place from where*:

Ἀθήνηθεν	from Athens
οἴκοθεν	from home
πανταχόθεν	from all directions

Space

The <u>accusative</u> is used to express *extent of space* (exactly like extent of time).

> *They marched for twenty stades.*
> εἴκοσι στάδια ἐπορεύθησαν.

> *The sea is two days' march away.*
> ἡ θάλασσα δύο σταθμοὺς ἀπέχει.

Note the following words:

στάδιον -ου τό	stade (*about 177.6 metres*)
σταθμός -οῦ ὁ	day's march

• Length, height and breadth are normally expressed by a genitive of the measurement and an accusative (of respect) for what it applies to.

> *a wall ten feet high* (lit. *of ten feet with respect to the height*)
> τεῖχος δέκα ποδῶν τὸ ὕψος

> *a road 100 stades long* (lit. *of 100 stades with respect to the length*)
> ὁδὸς ἑκατὸν σταδίων τὸ μῆκος

Note the following:

τὸ βάθος	in depth
τὸ εὖρος	in breadth
τὸ μῆκος	in length
τὸ ὕψος	in height

Exercises

A

1   The girls sailed to Athens on the next day.
2   I was waiting at home for many hours.
3   The Greeks were fighting there for ten years.
4   The messenger from the king of Persia is now here.
5   The old man saw the goddess just before nightfall.
6   Within three days we shall find out the truth.
7   The slaves were working for the whole night.
8   The contests happen every four years.
9   The gift was sent at the right time.
10 Odysseus returned home in the twentieth year.

B

1   At daybreak the soldiers arrived at a river 100 feet wide.
2   The king ruled for eight years.
3   We advanced one day's march.
4   I lived in the village for many months.
5   The harbour is nine stades from the city.
6   After this the woman went out of the house.
7   I soon found the money on the ground.
8   During the night we often heard shouts.
9   The soldier is carrying a spear twelve feet long.
10 I was writing for two hours but I did not send the letter.

Chapter 4: Use of adjectives

An adjective must agree with the noun to which it is attached in *number*, *gender*, and *case*.

• Any adjective can be made into a noun by adding an appropriate part of the definite article (from which a noun is supplied in English; when translating into Greek you should consider whether a word such as *men* or *things* is necessary).

the brave, brave men	*the wise woman*	*beauty*
οἱ ἀνδρεῖοι	ἡ σοφή	τὸ καλόν

• When an adjective is used with a noun, it is normally sandwiched with the article (or less commonly the article is repeated).

> *the stupid slave*
> ὁ μῶρος δοῦλος
> or ὁ δοῦλος ὁ μῶρος (lit. *the slave the stupid one*)

This is called the *bound* (the adjective is fastened to the noun) or *attributive* position (the adjective states an attribute of the noun).

There is however an important caution with the attributive use. In Greek *the stupid slave* necessarily implies a contrast with e.g. *the clever slave*: it serves to identify the slave in question. In English adjectives are often added to nouns more casually, to give colour, or to describe a person's character or behaviour on a particular occasion (rather than to contrast the person with someone else). In Greek here the adjective would have the present participle of εἰμί (ὤν οὖσα ὄν: see Chapter 6) added, or an adverb might be used instead.

> The stupid slave stole the wine.
> ὁ δοῦλος μῶρος ὤν ἔκλεψε τὸν οἶνον.

If the adjective is not joined to the noun like this (e.g. ὁ δοῦλος μῶρος or μῶρος ὁ δοῦλος) it is read as making a statement, with ἐστι supplied: *the slave is stupid*. This is called the *predicative* position (it predicates or states something new).

Comparative and superlative adjectives

An ordinary adjective (the form called the *positive*) tells us simply that the person or thing has the quality in question. To comment on the extent to which they have it, the *comparative* or *superlative* is used (these are called degrees of comparison).

• The comparative tells us that one person or thing has the quality to a greater extent than another. It is normally translated *X-er* or *more X* (the *-er* termination in used in English for adjectives of one syllable, and for some of two), typically followed by *than*.

• The superlative tells us that the person or thing has the quality to a very great extent, or to the greatest extent of any in a group. It is normally translated *very X, X-est* or *(the) most X.*

• The comparative is normally followed by ἤ *(than)*, with the two things being compared put in the same case.

> *The mother is much wiser than the daughter (is).*
> ἡ μήτηρ πολλῷ σοφωτέρα ἐστὶν ἢ ἡ θυγάτηρ.

Note the idiom πολλῷ *much* (neuter dative, literally *by much*), or πολύ (neuter accusative used adverbially), often attached to a comparative to stress how far one person or thing exceeds another in possession of the quality in question.

> *I gave a bigger prize to the old man than (I gave) to the young man.*
> ἔδωκα μεῖζον ἆθλον τῷ γέροντι ἢ τῷ νεανίᾳ.

• Alternatively, in a simple comparison ἤ may be omitted and the second item put in the genitive (the *genitive of comparison*), with the same meaning.

> ἡ μήτηρ πολλῷ σοφωτέρα ἐστὶν τῆς θυγατρός.

(The thought here is *by the side/standard of.*)

16

The comparative can also be used when no comparison is actually expressed, to mean *rather X* (more X than average) or *too X* (more X than required).

> *The book is rather/too long.*
> ἡ βίβλος μακροτέρα ἐστίν.

The superlative likewise is often free-standing.

> *The book is very long.*
> ἡ βίβλος μακροτάτη ἐστίν.

With the definite article it means *the X-est*, and is often followed by a genitive expressing the people or things surpassed.

> *the wisest of the Greeks*
> ὁ σοφώτατος τῶν Ἑλλήνων

Adverbs formed from adjectives

An adverb is formed from an adjective by changing the -ων of the genitive plural ending to -ως:

> *wise*   *wisely*
> σοφός, gen. pl. σοφῶν σοφῶς

The rule is put like this (rather than just changing the -ος or other last syllable of the nominative singular) to cope with examples where an epsilon on the stem is kept , e.g. ταχύς (*swift*), gen. pl. ταχέων, adverb ταχέως.

• The comparative adverb is the *neuter singular* of the comparative adjective.

> *The girl answered more wisely than the teacher.*
> ἡ παῖς σοφώτερον ἀπεκρίνατο ἢ ὁ διδάσκαλος.

• The superlative adverb is the *neuter plural* of the superlative adjective.

> *The politician always used to speak very wisely.*
> ὁ ῥήτωρ ἀεὶ σοφώτατα ἔλεγεν.

It is easy to see how this usage has come about: it is equivalent to *used to say very wise things.*

Note the idiom ὡς with a superlative (typically an adverb, but also possible with an adjective) to mean *as X as possible* (like *quam* with a superlative in Latin).

> *The allies arrived as quickly as possible.*
> οἱ σύμμαχοι ὡς τάχιστα ἀφίκοντο.

Exercises

A

1   The foolish young man did not obey the judge.
2   The book is new.
3   The girl is more skilful than all the boys.
4   The general spoke bravely but fought very bravely.
5   I chased the animals out of the field as quickly as possible.
6   The soldiers suffered more terribly than we did.
7   Beauty is admired by everyone.
8   The horse ran out of the sea quickly.
9   The most just of the citizens was killed.
10   The slave is much more trustworthy than the master.

B

1   The house is bigger than the temple.
2   The brave guard the weak.
3   We gave more food to the women than to the men.
4   The plan was better than the deed.
5   The giant is stronger than the sailors.
6   The slave answered more truthfully than the old man.
7   The easiest of the tasks is too difficult for me.
8   The Greeks were much wiser than the barbarians.
9   The soldiers were marching more slowly than the enemy.
10   Fools say many things but wise men are often silent.

Chapter 5: Verb tenses

This chapter gives more detail of regular usage which has been employed since the beginning of this book.

• The *present* tense describes an action that is happening now.

> *I run*   *we are eating*
> τρέχω   ἐσθίομεν

Greek does not distinguish by verb form *I run, I am running, I do run*.

• The *future* tense describes an action that has not yet happened.

> *you will send*   *they will hear*
> πέμψεις   ἀκούσονται

• The *imperfect* tense describes an action in the past that was incomplete, done repeatedly, or lasted a long time.

> *While we were waiting, the messenger arrived.*
> ἐν ᾧ ἐμένομεν, ὁ ἄγγελος ἀφίκετο.

> *The old man always used to speak like this.*
> ὁ γέρων ἀεὶ οὕτως ἔλεγεν.

> *I lived there for many years.*
> πολλὰ ἔτη ἐκεῖ ᾤκουν.

More specialised meanings are *I began to do X* and *I tried to do X*.

• The *aorist* tense describes a completed action in the past.

> *I sent the letter.*
> ἔπεμψα τὴν ἐπιστολήν.

• The *perfect* tense describes an action in the past whose effects continue.

> *I have learned all the words.*
> μεμάθηκα πάντας τοὺς λόγους.

The perfect is often virtually equivalent to a present tense.

The rare *pluperfect* tense describes something which had happened at an earlier stage and whose effects continued.

> *I had written previously.*
> πρότερον ἐγεγράφη.

In a subordinate clause describing one action which precedes another, Greek uses the aorist rather than the pluperfect (see Chapter 9 and Chapter 20).

> *When we (had) arrived, we set up camp.*
> ἐπεὶ ἀφικόμεθα, ἐστρατοπεδευσάμεθα.

• The present, future and perfect are *primary* tenses. The imperfect, aorist and pluperfect (which have the augment ἐ-) are *historic* tenses.

This distinction is important for constructions (e.g. purpose clause) which depend on *sequence* (see Chapter 14).

There are middle and passive versions of all the tenses. In the future and aorist, the middle and passive have different forms; in other tenses they are both the same. The middle has a range of uses: its name implies midway between active and passive, but in practice it often expresses something simultaneously active and passive, hence its *reflexive* use (e.g. λούομαι *I wash myself*) and its *causative* use (e.g. διδάσκομαι τὸν δοῦλον *I get the slave taught*). Verbs which exist only in a middle/passive form are called *deponent* (e.g. γίγνομαι *I become*). Tenses of deponent verbs are predominantly middle, but some prefer the passive form in the aorist (e.g. ἐπορεύθην *I marched*). Some ordinary verbs become deponent in the future (e.g. ἀκούσομαι *I shall hear*).

Passive verbs often have an *agent* (the person by whom the action is done), normally expressed by ὑπό and the genitive, and/or an *instrument* (the thing with which the action is done), expressed by the dative (see Chapter 1).

Exercises

A

1 The ships are sailing towards the harbour.
2 The disaster happened on the next day.
3 The prisoners will soon be released.
4 The girls have learned everything.
5 The men in the assembly will not listen to the speaker.
6 The slave was seen by the old man.
7 The battle had already ceased.
8 The allies have now arrived.
9 The women on the island were waiting for the messenger.
10 When I had returned home, I found the letter.

B

1 We lived in the house for ten years.
2 I always trust the words of the wise.
3 The gate was being guarded by four soldiers.
4 The girl has trained the horse well.
5 I finally got to know the truth.
6 The city will soon be captured.
7 Many women were waiting in the market-place.
8 The trees were cut down by the slaves.
9 The river will be dangerous in winter.
10 The teacher has written many books.

Chapter 6: Participles I

Greek has a full set of participles (present, future, aorist and perfect; active, middle and passive) and makes very full use of them: they are one of the most characteristic features of the language.

A participle does not have a tense in an absolute sense, but only in relation to the main verb of the sentence (hence a present participle describes something happening at the same time as the main verb, a future participle something which will happen later, and an aorist or perfect participle something which has happened already). In a typical narrative set in the past, a present participle represents the imperfect of a subordinate clause in English, and an aorist usually represents the pluperfect.

An aorist participle normally represents something which happens before (even if only momentarily before) the action of the main verb. In some idioms its use seems to be purely aspectual (like the aorist imperative or subjunctive), to describe a single act without reference to time: hence γελάσας ἔφη *he said with a laugh* (not necessarily before speaking). This must be distinguished from the more common situation where the aorist participle clearly does denote a prior action, but is represented by a present participle in English.

> *Hearing this, he left.*
> ταῦτα ἀκούσας ἀπῆλθεν

• A participle is an adjective made from a verb, and like any adjective can be used with the article to form a noun.

> *the man fleeing, the fugitive*
> ὁ φεύγων

• When a participle is used with a noun, there is an important distinction between the *circumstantial* use (what the person in question was doing at the time) and the use in *attributive* or *bound* position (normally with repeated article) to identify which person we are talking about (*the one who*).

The slave was wounded while running away.
ὁ δοῦλος ἀποτρέχων ἐτραυματίσθη.

The slave who was running away was wounded.
ὁ δοῦλος ὁ ἀποτρέχων ἐτραυματίσθη.

The circumstantial use replaces a temporal clause with *when* or *while* or a causal clause with *because* or *since*; the attributive use replaces a relative clause with *who* (see Chapter 9). Note that for the attributive use, the participle generally uses a repeated article to bind itself to the noun (rather than a sandwich, as ordinary adjectives more commonly do: see Chapter 4).

Genitive absolute

Participle phrases (noun plus participle) can be used in any case, according to the job being done in the sentence. But if a participle phrase is unconnected grammatically with the rest of the sentence (simply denoting an *attendant circumstance*, i.e. something else true or applicable at the time) it goes into the genitive: this is called the genitive absolute (in the original Latinate sense of *absolute* as *set free* or *independent*).

When the Athenians had fled, the people on the island rejoiced.
τῶν ᾿Αθηναίων φυγόντων, οἱ ἐν τῇ νήσῳ ἐχάρησαν.

As the danger is increasing, we want to retreat.
τοῦ κινδύνου αὐξανομένου, ἀναχωρῆσαι βουλόμεθα.

The genitive absolute corresponds to the ablative absolute in Latin, but is differently used because of the existence of a full set of participles. In particular, the availability of the aorist active participle makes it more easily able to replace a temporal or causal clause.

Exercises

A

1 The woman who has learned wisdom is fortunate.
2 The prisoner who had been released was captured again.
3 Those who have money are often admired.
4 The soldier was wounded while fighting.
5 The girls, who were brave, were guarding the wall all night.
6 The man who will lead us is still being sought.
7 Because the enemy had gone away, the citizens rejoiced.
8 I never heard about the things that had happened.
9 Seeing the market-place empty, we all went away.
10 The boy who had found the book later threw it away.

B

1 With few ships being here, we are in danger.
2 The gift sent by the king was very beautiful.
3 The book that is going to be written will be useful.
4 Because the food is bad, we are unwilling to stay.
5 The woman who is waiting here is getting angry.
6 Being wise, the old man says nothing.
7 We praise the things that were done then.
8 Because a shout had been heard, everyone was afraid.
9 The barbarians after killing a few men finally went away.
10 Because the water is bad, no-one now lives in the village.

Chapter 7: Pronouns I

Personal pronouns and possessives

Pronouns (words which stand in place of a noun and avoid the need to repeat it, e.g. *I, she, they*) are unusual in English in having a kind of declension (these examples changing after the nominative to *me, her, them*).

• First and second person pronouns in Greek (ἐγώ *I*, ἡμεῖς *we*, σύ *you* singular, ὑμεῖς *you* plural) are used in the nominative only for emphasis or to draw a contrast, because the verb ending already indicates the person.

> *I walk, but you run.*
> ἐγὼ μὲν βαδίζω, σὺ δὲ τρέχεις.

(See Chapter 10 for the use of μέν ... δέ to express a contrast.)

Note that the first person pronoun after the nominative has alternative forms: accusative ἐμέ or με, genitive ἐμοῦ or μου, dative ἐμοί or μοι. The version with the epsilon is more emphatic and must be used (1) if the pronoun comes first word in the sentence, (2) after a preposition, and (3) in a genitive absolute; the version without the epsilon is an enclitic and is used when it is felt to follow closely on the preceding word (e.g. πίστευέ μοι *believe me!*).

The associated possessives (ἐμός *my*, ἡμέτερος *our*, σός and ὑμέτερος *your*, i.e. of you singular and plural respectively) are adjectives and behave as such (see Chapter 4): they agree with a noun in number, gender and case (the gender that of the thing possessed). They normally have the article as well (because they specify a particular one), sandwiching the adjective or repeated, but this is not represented in English (see Chapter 2).

> *my books*   *your dog*   *our house*
> αἱ ἐμαὶ βίβλοι   ὁ σὸς κύων   ἡ ἡμετέρα οἰκία

When an adjective is available it is natural to use it, but it is also possible to use the genitive of the pronoun (*the X of me* rather than *my X*, in the case of the first person singular employing the enclitic form).

> *my brother*
> ὁ ἐμὸς ἀδελφός
> or   ὁ ἀδελφός μου

For a third person pronoun (*he, she, it, they*) Greek normally uses in the nominative the appropriate parts of the demonstrative pronouns *this* and *that* (see Chapter 8: literally *this man* etc), and for the other cases parts of αὐτός (see below).

For a third person possessive, there is an important distinction between the reflexive (*his [own]*, i.e. belonging to the subject of the sentence) and non-reflexive (*his* i.e. someone else's). For neither of these is there a commonly-used adjective. For the reflexive sense, if the reference is obvious, the norm is simply to use the article.

> *Oedipus killed his father.*
> ὁ Οἰδίπους ἀπέκτεινε τὸν πατέρα.

If an emphatic reflexive form is needed (*his/her <u>own</u>*), the genitive of the reflexive pronoun (ἑαυτοῦ -ῆς etc) is used. The non-reflexive possessive is the genitive of αὐτός. With both of these, the gender is that of the possessor.

simple reflexive:	*use the article*		
emphatic reflexive:	his (own) ἑαυτοῦ	her (own) ἑαυτῆς	their (own) ἑαυτῶν
non-reflexive:	his αὐτοῦ	her αὐτῆς	their αὐτῶν

Note carefully that the article (again redundant in English) is used with both of these, but <u>the reflexive version is sandwiched but the non-reflexive is not</u>:

The woman loves both her husband and his money, but hates her own brother.
ἡ γύνη φιλεῖ τόν τε ἄνδρα καὶ τὰ χρήματα αὐτοῦ, ἀλλὰ μισεῖ τὸν ἑαυτῆς ἀδελφόν.

The article alone can also be used as a first or second person possessive.
We love our native land.
φιλοῦμεν τὴν πατρίδα.

The genitives of first and second person reflexives are also used to mean *my/our/your* <u>own</u>. These reflexives (like third person ones) are sandwiched.
I killed my own mother.
ἀπέκτεινα τὴν ἐμαυτοῦ μητέρα.

The uses of αὐτός

This very important word has three different uses, which must be kept clearly distinct.

1   Meaning *self*

This is the sense of the obvious English derivatives (e.g. *automatic*). When used as a pronoun in the nominative it is not necessarily third person but agrees with the subject of the verb.

We ourselves won a victory.
αὐτοὶ ἐνικήσαμεν.

When used with a noun, it has the article (as the equivalent English also does) and is <u>not sandwiched</u>.

27

We saw the king himself.
εἴδομεν τὸν βασιλέα αὐτόν.

2 Meaning *the same*

This is always the meaning when part of αὐτός comes immediately after the definite article. It can be used as a pronoun.

They said the same things again.
τὰ αὐτὰ αὖθις εἶπον.

When it is used with a noun, this creates a sandwich.

The same messenger was sent.
ὁ αὐτὸς ἄγγελος ἐπέμφθη.

The use of αὐτός with a noun in senses (1) and (2) respectively thus normally gives the same word order as the equivalent English:

the general himself	*the same general*
ὁ στρατηγὸς αὐτός	ὁ αὐτὸς στρατηγός

The first could however less commonly be αὐτὸς ὁ στρατηγός: the important point is that it is not sandwiched.

3 Meaning *him, her, it, them*

This is always the meaning when part of αὐτός is used on its own as a pronoun and <u>not in the nominative</u>. It is always third person, and cannot come first word in a sentence or clause.

I saw her.
εἶδον αὐτήν.

We obeyed them.
ἐπιθόμεθα αὐτοῖς.

The non-reflexive possessive (αὐτοῦ etc) discussed above is the genitive of this.

Exercises

A

1   We are Greeks, you are barbarians.[1]
2   Three children have the same name.
3   My horse was being admired by everyone.
4   I led him into the camp.
5   The king himself will soon arrive.
6   Not my plan but yours will save the city, friend.
7   The teacher gave me his own book.
8   All the soldiers died on the same day.
9   The words themselves are not difficult.
10   I often saw her in the city.

[1] Use μέν ... δέ: see Chapter 10.

B

1   The slave always used to obey us.
2   The same woman was seen there again.
3   The general himself ordered us to flee.
4   I helped both the old man and his wife.
5   The messenger himself said the same things.
6   I do not know your name, boy.
7   The god himself replied to you.
8   The young man loved my sister.
9   Your houses were not being guarded, citizens.
10   The woman will not punish her own son.

Chapter 8: Pronouns II

The use of τίς and τις

This word has two distinct meanings, normally distinguished by accent (as well as word order).

1   Meaning *who?, what?, which?* (interrogative)

As a *question* word (see Chapter 12), all parts of τίς have an acute accent on the first or only syllable. It is invariably first word in the question (regardless of its case).

> *Who opened the door?*
> τίς ἀνέῳξε τὴν θύραν;

> *To whom did you send the letter?*
> τίνι ἔπεμψας τὴν ἐπιστολήν;

> *What happened?*
> τί ἐγένετο;

> *Which of the slaves answered?*
> τίς τῶν δούλων ἀπεκρίνατο;

• It can also be used as an adjective.

> *What name was given to her?*
> τί ὄνομα ἐδόθη αὐτῇ;

> *Which slave answered?*
> τίς δοῦλος ἀπεκρίνατο;

2   Meaning *a certain, a, someone, something, some* (indefinite)

As an *indefinite* (*a certain*, or just *a*, plural *some*), the monosyllabic parts of
τις normally have no accent but the two-syllable parts sometimes do. The
indefinite version too can be used on its own as a pronoun or with a noun
(which as an *enclitic* it follows); but even as a pronoun it <u>never comes first
word</u> in a sentence or clause. Hence as a pronoun:

> *Someone arrived.*
> ἀφίκετό τις.

> *We saw some people.*
> εἴδομέν τινας.

And as an adjective with a noun:

> *A certain slave arrived.*
> δοῦλός τις ἀφίκετο.

> *We saw some guards.*
> φύλακάς τινας εἴδομεν.

Note that a monosyllabic part of the indefinite τις may misleadingly acquire an
accent if it comes in front of another enclitic word, but the word order still leaves
no doubt that it is the indefinite and not the interrogative.
> *Give me something!*
> δός τί μοι.

Demonstratives

Words such as *this* and *that* (and more specialised ones like *so many*) are
called *demonstratives* because they point out or demonstrate (*this one here,
that one there*).

The usual Greek word for *this* is οὗτος αὕτη τοῦτο.

• Any part of οὗτος can be used on its own as a pronoun.

> *This woman is waiting.*
> αὕτη μένει.

> *He said these things.*
> εἶπε ταῦτα.

• It is regularly also used as an adjective with a noun, with the article (redundant in English), and <u>not sandwiched</u>.

> *This slave was punished.*
> οὗτος ὁ δοῦλος ἐκολάσθη.   (or ὁ δοῦλος οὗτος ...)

> *We love this girl.*
> φιλοῦμεν ταύτην τὴν παῖδα.

• An alternative (but less common) word for *this* is ὅδε ἥδε τόδε. Its use (on its own as a pronoun or with a noun and redundant article, and not sandwiched) is similar to that of οὗτος, but there is a preference for ὅδε when the emphasis is *this one actually here present*.

In one idiom the two words for *this* are contrasted (especially in the neuter plural): part of οὗτος typically refers back to something already mentioned, part of ὅδε forward to something about to be mentioned.
> *He announced these things* (already quoted/about to be quoted)
> ἤγγειλε ταῦτα / τάδε.

In form, ὅδε is simply the definite article with -δε stuck on the end.

• The word for *that* is ἐκεῖνος ἐκείνη ἐκεῖνο (from ἐκεῖ *there*, i.e. further away than something referred to as *this*. Its use (on its own as a pronoun or with a noun and redundant article, and not sandwiched) is again similar to that of οὗτος.

That man is asleep.
ἐκεῖνος καθεύδει.

I admire those books.
θαυμάζω ἐκείνας τὰς βίβλους.

• Note that either οὗτος or ἐκεῖνος can be used in the nominative simply for *he* etc.

The more specialised demonstratives τοσοῦτος (*so big*, plural *so many*) and τοιοῦτος (of such a sort), although formed like οὗτος, behave differently: they often have a redundant article, but are sandwiched.
   such a man
   ὁ τοιοῦτος ἀνήρ

Exercises

A

1   What shall we write?
2   Having said these things, the speaker sat down.
3   This goddess provided a very beautiful gift.
4   What happened after the sea battle?
5   That old man was very wise.
6   Who will dare to go into the forest at night?
7   I saw some children in the temple.
8   We received this letter yesterday.
9   Someone knows about these things.
10   I want to throw this book away.

B

1   A certain messenger came into the market-place.
2   This wine was praised by everyone.
3   Something fell out of the tree.
4   Whose is this dog?
5   I went out, but he stayed at home.[1]
6   We chased those horses into the field.
7   To whom shall I give the new book?
8   This woman is preparing the dinner.
9   That woman is guarding the wall.
10   Which slaves were sent to the city?

[1] Use μέν ... δέ (see Chapter 10).

Chapter 9: Relative clauses

The relative pronoun ὅς ἥ ὅ and the clause it introduces get their name from the fact that they *relate* or link two facts about a person or thing (as usual, the pronoun avoids the need to repeat a noun).

> *I admire the boy who received the prize.*
> θαυμάζω τὸν παῖδα ὃς ἐδέξατο τὸ ἆθλον.

The relative pronoun always has an accent (forms of it which are otherwise identical to parts of the definite article are distinguished in this way).

Note that like other pronouns (see Chapter 7) the relative changes its endings in English: the genitive *whose* is essential, though *whom* for other non-nominative cases is dropping out of use. English can also often use *that* or miss the relative out altogether (*the slave I saw*), but in Greek it is always put in.

• A relative clause in effect puts one sentence inside another. The sentence above is equivalent to *I admire the boy* plus *the boy/he received the prize*, i.e. the boy is the object in the first sentence and the subject in the second. When one sentence is put inside the other, each retains its own grammar. The relative pronoun therefore agrees with its *antecedent* (the noun in the main clause to which it refers back) in *number* and *gender*, but takes its *case* from the job it does in its own clause.

• Any combination of cases for antecedent and relative is possible.

> *The woman to whom I sent the letter is now here.*
> ἡ γυνὴ ᾗ ἔπεμψα τὴν ἐπιστολὴν νῦν πάρεστιν.
> (nominative antecedent, dative relative pronoun)

> *I will provide a meal for the children whose parents are away.*
> δεῖπνον παρέξω τοῖς παισὶν ὧν οἱ γονῆς ἄπεισιν.
> (dative antecedent, genitive relative pronoun)

I gave the book to the girl whom you saw yesterday.
ἔδωκα τὴν βίβλον τῇ παιδὶ ἣν χθὲς εἶδες.
(dative antecedent, accusative relative pronoun)

• When translating into Greek, think how the relative clause would operate as a separate sentence, and the case the relative pronoun needs to be in should be obvious.

The definite article with a participle is often used instead of a relative clause (see Chapter 6). Hence, going back to our first example:
I admire the boy who received the prize.
θαυμάζω τὸν παῖδα ὃς ἐδέξατο τὸ ἆθλον.
or   θαυμάζω τὸν παῖδα τὸν τὸ ἆθλον δεξάμενον.
Note that the participle (unlike the relative pronoun) agrees with the noun it refers to in *case* as well as in number and gender.

• Note that (as in temporal clauses: see Chapter 20) what English expresses as a pluperfect in a relative clause (*I released the men who had been captured*) is aorist in Greek.

• Although the relative pronoun is never missed out, the antecedent sometimes is (if it would simply be e.g. *he*, deducible from the number and gender of the antecedent).
He whom the gods love dies young.
ὃν οἱ θεοὶ φιλοῦσιν ἀποθνῄσκει νέος.

As an exception (upsetting the rule described above) note the phenomenon of *relative attraction*, whereby the magnetic force of a genitive or dative antecedent induces a relative pronoun that would have been accusative simply to follow suit.
I use the books which I have.
χρῶμαι ταῖς βίβλοις αἷς ἔχω.
(instead of the strictly correct ἃς ἔχω)

Omitted antecedent and relative attraction are often combined in a telescoped expression.

> *I shall ask her about the things she heard.*
> ἐρωτήσω αὐτὴν περὶ ὧν ἤκουσεν.
> (instead of περὶ τούτων ἃ ἤκουσεν)

Exercises

In these exercises use relative clauses (rather than article with participle).

A

1 The ship which you saw was sailing to Greece.
2 The goddess who received the prize is very beautiful.
3 I trust the doctor who wrote the letter.
4 We saw the soldiers who had arrived.
5 The boy hid the gold which he had found in the forest.
6 The prisoner who had fled was later seen by the old man.
7 The slave whom you sent is very stupid.
8 This is the girl whose name I do not know.
9 The gift which I received yesterday will be useful.
10 I announced these things to the citizens who were present.

B

1 We are seeking a leader who will be reliable.
2 You all saw the girl to whom I gave the prize.
3 We have a slave whose skill is admired by everyone.
4 Who is the speaker whose words we believe?
5 Socrates always used to obey the voice which he heard.
6 We were guarding the prisoners who had been captured.
7 I believe the words which the messenger spoke.
8 This is the sword with which I killed the giant.
9 I asked the boys about the things they had seen there.
10 The friend I had previously trusted betrayed me.

Chapter 10: Connection

Sentences in continuous narrative normally have connecting words, indicating how each sentence relates to the previous one (reinforcing it, explaining it, or introducing a contrary consideration). The most common connecting words are the following (those with an asterisk cannot come first word in a sentence or clause, but usually come second - i.e. immediately after the first word of the new sentence or clause, as if stitching the sentences together; they are technically called *post-positives*).

καί	and
ἀλλά	but
δέ*	and *or* but
οὖν*	therefore
μέντοι*	however
γάρ*	for
ὥστε	as a result
μέν* ... δέ*	on the one hand ... but on the other
τε* ... καί	both ... and
καί ... καί	both ... and
οὐ μόνον ... ἀλλὰ καί	not only ... but also

• Connecting words are used more often in Greek than in English to join sentences together. In a continuous passage they should normally be inserted, even if not explicitly present in the English version.

• Conversely *within* a sentence the use of a participle may eliminate an English connective.

Read and learn!
ἀναγνοὺς μαθέ.

Note that καί and ἀλλά can perfectly well begin sentences, without the restrictions which apply to the use of the equivalent words in English.

For a relatively colourless connection (which might be left untranslated when going from Greek to English), δέ can often be used. It is often appropriate to put it as second word in the very first sentence of a passage, signalling a link with what has gone before in the larger narrative from which the passage is assumed to be an extract.

A new clause after a colon (·), used also where English would have a semicolon or just a comma, is in effect a new sentence and thus normally has a connecting word.

> *The woman is miserable, for she has lost all her money.*
> ἡ γυνὴ δυστυχής ἐστιν· ἀπολώλεκε γὰρ πάντα τὰ χρήματα.

If no new subject is expressed, the subject is assumed to be the same as that of the previous sentence. Note the use of the article plus δέ to change the subject to someone mentioned in the previous sentence but not its subject.

> *I called the slave; but he did not hear.*
> ἐκάλεσα τὸν δοῦλον· ὁ δὲ οὐκ ἤκουσεν.

This is a fossilised survival of the use in pre-classical Greek of the article as a pronoun (see Chapter 2).

If ὥστε starts a sentence, it means *as a result* (or similar); more commonly it introduces a result clause (see Chapter 15) within a sentence, with a preceding signpost word (e.g. τοσοῦτος ... ὥστε *so big ... that*).

Greek authors very frequently use μέν ... δέ to express a contrast. The equivalent English will often have nothing for μέν, and *while/whilst* or *but* for δέ.

> *The Athenians stayed, whilst the Spartans fled.*
> οἱ μὲν ᾿Αθηναῖοι ἔμειναν, οἱ δὲ Λακεδαιμόνιοι ἔφυγον.

Note carefully that μέν and δέ *co-ordinate*, i.e. join together two items of equal weight (typically two main clauses): they cannot connect (for example) a time clause or participle phrase with a main clause. Note also that μέν looks forward to the following δέ and does not link back to the previous sentence, and therefore often occurs together with another connective (typically οὖν or γάρ).

> *The Athenians therefore stayed ...*
> οἱ μὲν οὖν ᾿Αθηναῖοι ἔμειναν ...

For the idiom οἱ μέν ... οἱ δέ (*some ... others*) see Chapter 2.

Both τε ... καί and καί ... καί can join clauses as well as individual words or phrases. Note that because τε is a post-positive, it comes second word within the first of the two items being joined; it will end up next to καί only if the first item is a single word.

> *both the body and the soul* *I both teach and learn.*
> τό τε σῶμα καὶ ἡ ψυχή διδάσκω τε καὶ μανθάνω.

Exercises

A

A certain philosopher was living in Athens. Since he was poor, this man never locked his house. Once a thief came in during the night, while the philosopher was sleeping; for he wanted to steal money. Because he found nothing, however, he became angry. As a result the philosopher heard him shouting. Then he said 'Be quiet[1], friend! For I, who live here, am not able to find money during the day. Therefore you, who are a stranger, will scarcely find money during the night.'

[1] Use the imperative (see Chapter 13).

B

Croesus was king of the Lydians. He had a son whom he very greatly loved; and indeed, this young man was both bravest and best of all the ones at that time. His father, however, in a dream saw him wounded by a spear. He therefore decided to guard the boy at home. The king also took out the weapons from the house. But all these things were done in vain. For his son wanted to go hunting and finally persuaded his father. In this way therefore he was allowed to go out. Soon, however, he was accidentally hit by a certain friend's spear and died.

PART 2

Chapter 11: Indirect statement

An indirect statement occurs when what someone *says, thinks, sees, hears, knows* etc. is reported by another. In English the subordinate clause is regularly introduced by *that*, though this is sometimes omitted.

Direct statement

The citizens are fleeing.
The general will soon come.
The sailors have arrived.

Indirect statement

He says <u>that</u> the citizens are fleeing.
We said <u>that</u> the general would soon come.
She knew the sailors had arrived.

In Greek there are <u>three</u> different constructions for dealing with indirect statements.

1   The ὅτι or ὡς construction

This construction is regularly used after verbs of *saying,* especially λέγω and its aorist εἶπον, ἀποκρίνομαι and ἀγγέλλω. It <u>must not</u> be used after φημί or verbs of *thinking* (νομίζω and οἴομαι).

• The word ὅτι or ὡς (or sometimes ὅπως) is used to translate the English *that.*

• The verb in the indirect statement retains the mood and tense of the original direct speech, i.e. the same mood and tense as the original speaker used.

• In historic sequence (i.e. after a main verb in a past tense, usually imperfect or aorist) the optative may be used, though the tense will still be that of the original direct speech. The optative in sentences like this is less vivid than the indicative.

• The negative is regularly οὐ.

> *He says that the soldiers are staying in their camp.*
> λέγει ὅτι οἱ στρατιῶται μένουσιν ἐν τῷ στρατοπέδῳ.

> *The slave announced that the boy had fallen into a river*
> ὁ δοῦλος ἤγγειλεν ὅτι ὁ παῖς ἔπεσεν εἰς ποταμόν.

> *He said that the boy was stupid.*
> εἶπεν ὅτι ὁ παῖς μῶρος εἴη (or μῶρός ἐστιν).

> *They answered that his father would be very angry.*
> ἀπεκρίναντο ὅτι ὁ πατὴρ αὐτοῦ μάλιστα ὀργιεῖται.

As in the second example above, the aorist is regularly used to represent the English pluperfect in an historic indirect statement.

After many verbs expressing emotion (particularly θαυμάζω *I am surprised that*, ἀγανακτέω *I am indignant that*, and ἀγαπάω *I am content that*) εἰ is often used instead of ὅτι; negative μή.
> *I am surprised that none of you wants to read this book.*
> θαυμάζω εἰ μηδεὶς ὑμῶν ἐθέλει ἀναγνῶναι ταύτην τὴν βίβλον.

The infinitive construction

After φημί and verbs of *thinking* (especially νομίζω and οἴομαι) the verb in an indirect statement goes into the infinitive.

• The tense of the infinitive corresponds to that of the original words of the direct statement. Thus, in historic sequence, the present infinitive is used to represent an English imperfect indicative, whilst for the pluperfect, although the perfect infinitive sometimes occurs, the aorist is more regularly found.

• If the subject of the indirect statement is different from that of the main verb, it will be in the accusative (exactly as in the equivalent Latin construction).

• If it is the same, it is usually not expressed, but will be in the nominative if it is included.

• The negative is regularly οὐ. Note that *say that ... not* is οὐ φημί, and *think that ... not* is οὐκ οἴομαι or οὐ νομίζω.

> *The doctor thought that the boy was ill.*
> ὁ ἰατρὸς ἐνόμιζε τὸν παῖδα νοσεῖν.

> *The young man said that he wanted to be a teacher.*
> ὁ νεανίας ἔφη βούλεσθαι διδάσκαλος γενέσθαι.

> *The guard said that not he himself but his wife had opened the gates.*
> ὁ φύλαξ οὐκ ἔφη αὐτὸς ἀλλὰ τὴν γυναῖκα ἀνοῖξαι τὰς πύλας.

Note that in the final example above αὐτός, referring back to the subject of the main verb, is nominative, whilst τὴν γυναῖκα, someone else, is accusative.

ἐλπίζω *I hope*, ὑπισχνέομαι *I promise*, ὄμνυμι *I swear* and ἀπειλέω *I threaten* are generally followed by a future infinitive. The negative is μή.
> *They promised not to kill the king.*
> = *They promised that they wouldn't kill the king.*
> ὑπέσχοντο μὴ ἀποκτενεῖν τὸν βασιλέα.

The negative is also regularly μή when verbs which express a 'confident assertion' use the infinitive construction. Such verbs are πιστεύω *I trust*, μαρτύρομαι *I testify*, διϊσχυρίζομαι *I assert* and the perfect passive πέπεισμαι *I am convinced*.
> *I assert that such a disaster will never happen again.*
> διϊσχυρίζομαι τὴν τοιαύτην συμφορὰν μηδέποτε αὖθις γενήσεσθαι.

The participle construction

Indirect statements after verbs of *knowing* and *perceiving*, and a few others, are regularly expressed with a participle rather than an infinitive.

• Just as with the infinitive construction, if the subject of the indirect statement is the same as that of the main verb, it is either omitted or is in the nominative; if different, it is in the accusative.

• The participle agrees with its subject in the normal way.

• The negative is οὐ.

The most common verbs which take this construction are:

οἶδα	I know
ἐπίσταμαι	I know, understand
σύνοιδα ἐμαυτῷ	I am conscious
ἀγνοέω	I don't know
γιγνώσκω	I get to know, realise
μανθάνω	I learn, get to know
πυνθάνομαι	I ascertain, find out
αἰσθάνομαι	I perceive (*with acc. or gen.*)
εὑρίσκω	I find out
ὁράω	I see
ἀκούω	I hear
δηλόω	I show
δείκνυμι	I show, point out
(ἀπο)φαίνω	I show, reveal
μέμνημαι	I remember (*with gen.*)
ἐπιλανθάνομαι	I forget (*with gen.*)
ἀγγέλλω	I announce

Pericles knows that this young man is a friend.
ὁ Περικλῆς οἶδε τοῦτον τὸν νεανίαν φίλον ὄντα.

He realised that he was making a big mistake.
ἔγνω μάλιστα ἁμαρτάνων.

I am conscious that I have many enemies here.
σύνοιδα ἐμαυτῷ πολλοὺς ἐνθάδε ἔχων (or ἔχοντι) ἐχθρούς.

The ὅτι construction may be used with many of these verbs, particularly οἶδα and ἐπίσταμαι, when used in the context of knowledge of a fact.
And this I do know for sure, that Philip is approaching at speed.
καὶ τοῦτο σαφῶς δὴ οἶδα, ὅτι ὁ Φίλιππος κατὰ τάχος προσέρχεται.

When the verb of *knowing* or *perceiving* is itself a participle, it is commonly followed by the ὅτι construction.
Realising that the enemy were approaching, the general took to flight.
γνοὺς ὅτι οἱ πολέμιοι προσχωροῖεν, ὁ στρατηγὸς ἐς φυγὴν κατέστη.

Exercises

A   (ὅτι construction only)

1   That messenger announced that the enemy ships were approaching.
2   The girl replied that she would soon be present herself.
3   The scouts said that the barbarians had fled towards the river.
4   The children were saying with a shout (= shouting) that their friends were in great danger.
5   Phidippides soon arrived with the news (= announcing) that Darius had been defeated at Marathon.
6   I am very surprised that your parents allow you to play in the road.
7   The king replied that he wished to make the Greeks his friends.
8   All who were present said that no one had done wrong intentionally.
9   The general asserted that his men would encamp for the night near the sea.
10   My friend says that he will come to my assistance tomorrow.

B   (ὅτι and infinitive constructions)

In this exercise translate the verb to say *by* φημί *throughout.*

1   These boys say that they found the money in the wood.
2   We think that the Spartans are the bravest of all the Greeks.
3   The orator replied that he was trying to persuade the citizens to vote for war.
4   The students said that they would never give their written work to the teacher.
5   Those slaves threatened to hand over our city to the barbarians immediately.
6   Socrates always used to say that the soul was immortal.
7   The fugitives hoped to escape from the city unharmed; however they were betrayed, captured and thrown into prison once again.
8   The Greeks always thought that it was just to honour those who had died in battle.
9   Themistocles announced to the assembly that the Athenians had to put their trust in the navy.
10   The traitors' leader trusted that his friends would never reveal his secret.

C   (all three constructions)

1   I know that my friend is travelling here from Athens today.
2   The priest saw that he had arrived at the temple.
3   Wise men know well that kings are not happy.
4   Realising that the children were ill, their father quickly sent for a doctor.
5   The defeated soldiers said that not they themselves but their general was responsible for the disaster.
6   The herald announced that the king's son was already dead.
7   We knew perfectly well that those slaves were not going to tell the truth.
8   He promised to leave no stone unturned in his search for (= seeking) those who had wronged his father.

9   The Athenians perceived that the Persians wished to attack Attica by both land and sea.

10   The envoys replied that they had promised to persuade the citizens to accept these proposals.

D

When news arrived in Athens[1] that the fleet had been destroyed in Sicily, the citizens at first disbelieved it; but later, when the matter became clear, they grew angry with the politicians who had supported[2] the expedition. For, deprived now of both cavalry and infantry, and at the same time seeing neither ships in their harbours nor money in their public treasury, they could no longer have any expectation of deliverance[3]. And they also thought that their enemies from Sicily would soon attack them by sea, whilst the rest would immediately invade Attica by land. And the city was full of uproar. Nevertheless, gathering together both timber and money, they resolved to get a new fleet ready; and in addition they chose a council of elders, as they knew perfectly well that the whole assembly would never be able to curtail the current panic.

[1] When news arrived in Athens = When it was reported into Athens.

[2] I support: συμπροθυμέομαι (*aor.* συμπρούθυμήθην) with accusative.

[3] ... could no longer have any expectation of deliverance = could no longer hope to be saved.

Chapter 12: Questions

Direct questions

There are five main ways of introducing normal direct questions in Greek. In all of them the verb is in the indicative.

1   Interrogative word

When a question begins with an interrogative word in English, it is likely to begin in Greek with one of the words from the following list. Note that the first five words in the list decline and must be put in the correct form, according to their role in the sentence and the words they qualify. The rest are indeclinable, i.e. never change.

who? what?	τίς τί (see Chapter 8)
which (of two)?	πότερος -α -ον
what sort of?	ποῖος -α -ον
how great, how big?	πόσος -η -ον
how many?	πόσοι -αι -α
from where, whence?	πόθεν
where?	ποῦ
where to, whither?	ποῖ
when?	πότε
how?	πῶς
why?	τί, διὰ τί

Who is approaching?   *What are they doing?*
τίς προσχωρεῖ;   τί ποιοῦσιν;

How many fish did you catch?   *Where did the sailor go?*
πόσους ἔλαβες ἰχθῦς;   ποῖ ἦλθεν ὁ ναυτής;

2   ἆρα

A question introduced by ἆρα simply seeks information, with no implication as to the expected answer. It turns a statement into a question.

The girl loves her dog.　　　　　*Does the girl love her dog?*
ἡ παῖς φιλεῖ τὸν κύνα.　　　　ἆρα ἡ παῖς φιλεῖ τὸν κύνα;

ἦ is sometimes used for ἆρα, particularly in verse.

ἆρα may be omitted, and the question indicated simply by the question mark (;).

ἄλλο τι or ἄλλο τι ἤ may be used to express *Is it the case that* ...
　　　　Is it the case that the girl loves her dog?
　　　　ἄλλο τι ἤ ἡ παῖς φιλεῖ τὸν κύνα;

3　　οὐκοῦν, ἆρ᾽ οὐ

Questions introduced by οὐκοῦν or ἆρ᾽ οὐ (ἆρα οὐ), or just by οὐ, expect
the answer *yes*, though that may not be the answer actually given.

　　　　Doesn't the girl love her dog?
　　　　The girl does love her dog, doesn't she?
　　　　Surely the girl loves her dog?
　　　　οὐκοῦν ἡ παῖς φιλεῖ τὸν κύνα;

4　　μή, ἆρα μή, μῶν

Questions introduced by any of these (ἆρα μή is particularly uncommon)
expect the answer *no*, though again that may not be the answer actually
given.

　　　　The girl doesn't love her dog, does she?
　　　　Surely the girl doesn't love her dog?
　　　　μῶν ἡ παῖς φιλεῖ τὸν κύνα;

5　　**Alternative (double) questions**

These are introduced by πότερον (or πότερα), followed later in the
sentence by ἤ (= *or*). The πότερον a) may be left out, and b) mustn't be
translated: it is simply an indication that a second part of the question is on
the way. *Or not* is ἤ οὔ.

Do you wish to travel to Athens or to Thebes?
(πότερον) βούλει πορεύεσθαι Ἀθήναζε ἢ Θήβαζε;

Does the student want to read the book or not?
πότερον βούλεται ὁ μαθητὴς ἀναγνῶναι τὴν βίβλον ἢ οὔ;

Deliberative questions

These are questions where the speaker asks what he <u>is to do</u>, or <u>was to do</u>. They are expressed in Greek by the subjunctive, present or aorist; negative μή. When there is no interrogative word, they may, but need not, be introduced by βούλει or βούλεσθε.

What am I to say?   *Am I to say this?*
τί εἴπω;   [βούλει] εἴπω ταῦτα;

They may also be expressed by using the impersonal verbs δεῖ or χρή. This is particularly the case when they refer to past time.

What are we to do?   *What were we to do?*
τί δεῖ [ἡμᾶς] ποιεῖν;   τί ἔδει [ἡμᾶς] ποιεῖν;

Indirect questions

Indirect questions in Greek use essentially the same construction as indirect statements of the ὅτι variety.

• The regular pattern is introductory verb (typically *ask, know, find out*) followed by a clause starting with an interrogative word, and with its verb in the same mood and tense as the original direct question.

• As with indirect statements, in historic sequence the optative may be used, but still in the same tense as the original direct question.

• The direct interrogatives on page 48 may always be used, but it is also possible to use their indirect forms. These are formed by adding ὁ- to the direct form, e.g. ὁποῖος, ὁπότε, ὅποι etc.

• τίς becomes ὅστις. It needs special attention as both parts of the word decline.

• εἰ is used to mean *if, whether*. (ὁ)πότερον should be used only in the first part of a double question, and ἐάν should never be used.

• εἴτε ... εἴτε is a possible alternative to (ὁ)πότερον ... ἤ in a double question.

• The negative is regularly οὐ, but may be μή after εἰ and in ἢ μή (*or not*) in the second part of a double question.

> *The boy asks where his mother is.*
> ὁ παῖς ἐρωτᾷ ὅπου ἐστὶν ἡ μήτηρ.

> *We could not find out why the woman was crying.*
> οὐκ ἐδυνάμεθα πυθέσθαι διὰ τί ἡ γυνὴ δακρύοι.

> *The innkeeper asked whether we wanted to enter or not.*
> ὁ πανδοκεὺς ἤρετο πότερον βουλοίμεθα εἰσιέναι ἢ μή.

The verb *to ask* which introduces an indirect question is ἐρωτάω. As well as its regular forms, it has an alternative future, ἐρήσομαι, and an alternative aorist, ἠρόμην.

The subject of an indirect question sometimes appears as the object of the main verb (though not after verbs of *asking*, and rarely after negatives).
> *I know who the sailor is.*
> = *I know the sailor, who he is.*
> οἶδα τὸν ναύτην ὅστις ἐστίν.

When a deliberative question becomes indirect, the verb may always remain in the subjunctive, but, in historic sequence, may become optative. It is worth observing that the only place where the subjunctive is found in Greek indirect questions is in indirect deliberative questions. Of course δεῖ and χρή may still be used to achieve the same sense.

> *They didn't know what they were to do.*
> οὐκ ᾔδεσαν τί ποιήσωσιν (or ποιήσειαν).
> or οὐκ ᾔδεσαν τί δεῖ (or δέοι) ποιῆσαι.

Indirect questions are often the best way of translating English abstract nouns, e.g. *size, character, number* etc. (This is the case in Latin also.)

> *I asked him about his father's character.*
> ἠρόμην αὐτὸν ὁποῖος εἴη ὁ πατήρ.

> *We know the size of the city.*
> ἴσμεν τὴν πόλιν ὁπόση ἐστίν.

Exercises

A (direct questions only)

1   What kind of books does your brother read?
2   Why do you not want to go to the theatre with me?
3   Does your mother like the poems of Homer?
4   Surely these are the horses which your grandfather was trying to give me?
5   Does Evenus intend to remain for some time in the city, or to return home immediately?
6   Surely the Athenians didn't obey the Spartan king willingly?
7   What am I to say to you? How many Spartans did you see combing their hair?
8   Were we not to preserve these tables which our ancestors bequeathed to us?
9   Whom did you stop in the street? Where was he going and why did he not want to talk to you?

10 Are not these slaves deserving of a very serious punishment?

B (indirect questions only)

1 I asked the captain why he had not reported the matter to me after the battle.
2 They want to find out not only where that merchant lives, but also what kind of things he sells.
3 Socrates used to go around asking the citizens if they thought they were wise.
4 All wanted to know why the teacher had written such a letter.
5 They asked each of the cavalrymen whether in any way (τι) he had helped the Athenians in the war.
6 I do not know what type of things my friend is doing in Italy.
7 We shall soon find out which of the two thieves is responsible for this murder.
8 We asked the strangers who they were and where they were travelling to.
9 The enemy knew neither the extent of the danger nor what kind of ships the Syracusans had.
10 For a long time indeed the Athenians were at a loss (as to) how they were to save both their city and their citizens.

C (direct and indirect questions; revision of indirect statement)

1 He surely doesn't say that those who seek after pleasure are good men?
2 We know why the citizens were surrendering the city to the barbarians.
3 We threatened to ask why the authorities wished to destroy the school.
4 Xenophon's soldiers asked the guide whether he had lost his way.
5 The scouts reported what kind of ships they had seen in the harbour and how many marines would soon attack our city.
6 My girlfriend told me the amount of money she had for (*use* πρός *with accusative*) her trip abroad.

7   The young man decided to find out whether there were bats in the tower or not.

8   My father says that yesterday the slaves did not give water either to the horses or to the oxen.

9   It isn't easy for anyone to form an estimation of the character of Alcibiades.

10   The Athenians do not yet realise the extent of the force which Xerxes is intending to send.

D

Since night had now descended[1] on them, Philip and his band of followers[2] found a suitable spot and made their camp; and when they had had a meal, they soon lay down to sleep[3]. But it chanced that nearby there was a large and frightening castle[4] in which dwelt an evil giant. In the morning he went out and found the Greeks sleeping on his land. He woke them up and angrily asked who they were, where they came from and what their business was. They said that they were Greeks who were travelling to the coast but had lost their way. 'But now', said the giant, 'you must come with me to my castle; for in trampling[5] on my land like this you do me an injustice, and deserve a very serious penalty.' 'What then', said Philip, 'are you going to do? For we are guilty of nothing but ignorance.' But the giant said nothing in reply. When they reached the castle, the Greeks were cast into a dark dungeon; and there they remained for four days without food and drink, and far from[6] their friends.

[1] descended: use ἐπέρχομαι.

[2] Philip and his band of followers = οἱ ἀμφὶ τὸν Φίλιππον.

[3] lay down to sleep: use κοιμάομαι.

[4] castle: use πύργος.

[5] I trample on: καταπατέω (with accusative).

[6] far from: πόρρω ἀπό (with genitive).

Chapter 13: Commands, exhortations and wishes

Commands

Second-person and third-person commands are expressed by the imperative. The present imperative is used for general commands, the aorist for specific instructions.

> *Always obey your father.*
> πείθου ἀεὶ τῷ πατρί.

> *Come here.*
> ἐλθὲ δεῦρο.

> *Let the people sing.*
> ᾀδόντων οἱ ἄνθρωποι.

> *Let him go away now.*
> ἀπελθέτω νῦν.

Negative commands are known as **prohibitions**. General prohibitions are expressed by μή with the present imperative. Particular prohibitions use μή with the aorist subjunctive.

> *Do not steal.*
> μὴ κλέπτετε.

> *Do not do this.*
> μὴ τοῦτο ποιήσῃς.

A second negative command is introduced by μηδέ if the first command is negative; or by καὶ μή if the first command is positive.

> *Don't bring your friends here or make a noise in the house.*
> μὴ ἄγετε δεῦρο τοὺς φίλους μηδὲ θορυβεῖτε ἐν τῇ οἰκίᾳ.

> *Wait here and don't annoy your mother.*
> ἐνθάδε μεῖνον καὶ μὴ λυπήσῃς τὴν μητέρα.

ὅπως and ὅπως μή with the future indicative may be used to express commands and prohibitions.

> *Kill the king.*
> ὅπως ἀποκτενεῖς τὸν βασιλέα.

> *Don't do this.*
> ὅπως μὴ τοῦτο ποιήσεις.

First-person commands are known as **exhortations**. Greek uses the present or aorist subjunctive: present for general, aorist for particular. The negative is μή.

Let us always love our fatherland.   *Let's not do this.*
ἀεὶ φιλῶμεν τὴν πατρίδα.   μὴ τοῦτο ποιήσωμεν.

Wishes

Wishes for the future are expressed by εἴθε or εἰ γάρ followed by the optative, present or aorist. εἴθε and εἰ γάρ may be omitted. The negative is μή.

May you be luckier than your father!   *May it not happen!*
εἰ γὰρ εὐτυχέστερος εἴης τοῦ πατρός.   (εἴθε) μὴ γένοιτο.

Wishes for the present have the imperfect indicative after εἴθε or εἰ γάρ, those for the past the aorist indicative. εἴθε and εἰ γάρ may not be omitted. The negative is μή.

If only the boy were not doing this!   *If only he had done this!*
εἴθε μὴ τοῦτο ἐποίει ὁ παῖς.   εἰ γὰρ τοῦτο
          ἐποίησεν.

Wishes for the present and past may be expressed also by ὤφελον (aorist of ὀφείλω) followed by either the present or aorist infinitive. εἴθε, εἰ γάρ or ὡς may precede the required part of ὤφελον. The negative is μή.

If only my parents were here!   *Would that he had seen us!*
ὤφελον παρεῖναι οἱ γονῆς μου.   ὤφελεν ἡμᾶς ἰδεῖν.

Indirect commands

These are expressed in Greek by the infinitive, just as in English. The negative is μή.

The teacher told the students to read three books.
ὁ διδάσκαλος ἐκέλευσε τοὺς μαθητὰς τρεῖς ἀναγνῶναι βίβλους.

Verbs regularly followed by this construction are:

κελεύω	I order
λέγω with dative	I tell, order
νουθετέω	I warn
παραινέω with dative	I advise
αἰτέω	I ask, beg
ἀξιόω	I ask, beg, urge
δέομαι with genitive	I ask
πείθω	I persuade
παρακελεύομαι with dative	I encourage
παραμυθέομαι with dative	I exhort

Greek likes, where possible, to have an active infinitive after κελεύω.
He ordered the prisoners to be set free.
= He gave orders to set free the prisoners.
ἐκέλευσεν ἐλευθερῶσαι τοὺς αἰχμαλώτους.

Subordinate clauses in indirect speech

All clauses dependent on indirect statements, questions or commands, if they are part of the original thought, follow these rules.

• If the main verb is primary, the mood and tense of the verb in the subordinate clause do not change.

All teachers will advise their pupils to read the book which I wrote.
πάντες διδάσκαλοι παραινέσουσι τοῖς μαθηταῖς ἀναγνῶναι
τὴν βίβλον ἣν ἔγραψ᾽ ἐγώ.

• If the main verb is historic, either the mood and tense of the original direct speech are retained in the subordinate clause, or the tense is retained and the mood becomes optative. The historic tenses of the indicative, particularly the aorist, should not be so changed.

He said that the children whom they were capturing would reveal all.
ἔφη τοὺς παῖδας οὓς λαμβάνουσι/λαμβάνοιεν πάντα μηνύσειν.

He said that the children whom they had captured would reveal all.
ἔφη τοὺς παῖδας οὓς ἔλαβον πάντα μηνύσειν.

Exercises

A

1 Love the gods, young men, and honour your parents.
2 Do not send this letter to your mother; for she will be very irritated indeed when she reads it (= having read it).
3 Let us fight bravely and worthily of our ancestors.
4 Come in at once, and tell me why you are wearing such strange clothes.
5 Let them send the triremes out of the harbour now; for the storm is no longer frightening.
6 If only my grandfather were here! For he understands all these things well.
7 May his father never know that his son is such a criminal!
8 Let us never imagine, citizens, that this war is just. May the truce remain for many years!
9 Do nothing disgraceful, my friend; for the gods see everything everywhere.
10 Let the slave go off to the field and untie the oxen.

B

1 I warn you, my boy, not to think that I am a stupid old man.
2 The mother used to advise her daughters never to talk to strange men.

3   If only there could be more women in the government!

4   My friend, give the gold which you have to the poor, and do not conceal it in your house.

5   Do not cross the road with your eyes closed, you fool; for the danger is very great.

6   May this truce not be broken, nor the mob put its trust in evil politicians.

7   If only I had perished while fighting against the Syracusans in the harbour! For quarrying stones doesn't appeal to me at all.

8   Tomorrow I'm going to ask my friend's sister to marry me.

9   Always fight bravely, and never throw away your shield.

10   Let virtue never be thought disgraceful among men, but let it be (held) in the highest honour.

C

1   Themistocles was constantly persuading the Athenians to go on board their ships.

2   Ask Alcibiades if he knows where the house of the flute-girl is.

3   The judge promised to release the prisoners whom he was trying.

4   The captain ordered the wicked sailors to be thrown into the sea.

5   My brother's solicitor advised him to go to law about the matter.

6   I know that it is my sister whom you consider the most beautiful of all women.

7   I beg you not to be afraid of my dog; for he is very tame and never bites those who stroke him.

8   I asked my son to disclose to me where he had hidden the wine which he had stolen.

9   I shall try to persuade my friends not to travel to foreign parts; however I do not think that they will be willing listen to (= obey) me.

10   Demosthenes ordered the officers to put to death at once the Spartans whom they had arrested.

D

Croesus, king of the Lydians, ruled over many peoples and had very great wealth, but was nevertheless always unhappy because his son was deaf and dumb. Accordingly he once travelled to Delphi, wishing to consult the oracle about the boy, and immediately on his arrival went into the temple, and bursting into tears said[1], 'If only my son were endowed with speech[2]! What must I do to hear him speaking[3]?' But the Pythia replied as follows: 'You will only hear your son's voice when a huge disaster falls upon the state[4].' Some time later, when Sardis was being taken by the Persians, one of the enemy was about to kill the king, ignorant of who he was. When Croesus saw him coming, he said with a groan, 'Let the enemy attack me, and let my empire be destroyed; for I no longer wish to live.' But his dumb son saw that his father was in great danger, and with an unexpected shout said, 'Be off with you, you wretch, and don't kill the king.' Thus he first used his voice, and everyone realised that the god's words were true.

[1] bursting into tears (he) said: in circumstances like this use an aorist participle of the appropriate verb before the required part of φημί, = δακρύσας ἔφη. There are two other comparable cases later in the passage.

[2] endowed with speech = φωνήεις -εσσα -εν.

[3] What must I do to hear him speaking? = Having done what (τί ποιήσας) will I hear him speaking?

[4] when a huge disaster falls upon the state: use a genitive absolute here = a huge disaster having fallen upon the state.

Chapter 14: Purpose clauses

Purpose clauses, often referred to as final clauses, are introduced in English by *to*, *in order to*, *so as to*, etc., as in the following example:

to see the Parthenon.
We travelled to Athens in order to see the Parthenon.
so as to see the Parthenon.

In Greek there are three main ways of expressing purpose.

1   The ἵνα construction

The conjunctions ἵνα, ὅπως or ὡς introduce a clause whose verb is subjunctive in primary sequence, optative in historic sequence. But in historic sequence, by the so-called 'vivid construction', the subjunctive may be used rather than the optative.

• The present subjunctive and optative are used for continuous or repeated action, the aorist for individual or single action.

• The negative is μή, either on its own, or (more normally) following ἵνα, ὅπως or ὡς.

> *We read many books in order to become wise.*
> πολλὰς ἀναγιγνώσκομεν βίβλους ἵνα σοφοὶ γιγνώμεθα.
>
> *The troops were fighting bravely in order to capture the harbour.*
> οἱ στρατιῶται ἀνδρείως ἐμάχοντο ἵνα λάβοιεν/λάβωσι τὸν λιμένα.
>
> *I departed at once in order not to see my brother's wife.*
> εὐθὺς ἀπῆλθον (ἵνα) μὴ ἴδοιμι τὴν τοῦ ἀδελφοῦ γυναῖκα.

ἄν is sometimes found with ὡς or ὅπως and the subjunctive.

> *I am teaching you this so that you may have a possession for ever.*
> ταῦτα διδάσκω ὑμᾶς ὡς ἂν ἔχητε κτῆμα ἐς αἰεί.

ἵνα with a past tense of the indicative expresses an unfulfilled purpose, especially after an unfulfilled condition or an unaccomplished wish; negative μή.

> *If only my father had died in the war, so that he might never have seen the Persian victory!*
> εἴθε ἀπέθανεν ὁ πατήρ μου ἐν τῷ πολέμῳ, ἵνα μήποτε εἶδε τὴν τῶν Περσῶν νίκην.

2   The future participle

The future participle is regularly used to express purpose, often in conjunction ὡς.

> *They led away the prisoners in order to put them to death.*
> ἀπήγαγον τοὺς αἰχμαλώτους ὡς ἀποκτενοῦντες.

• ὡς is usually omitted with verbs of motion.

> *They came to Athens to see the Parthenon.*
> ἦλθον Ἀθήναζε ὀψόμενοι τὸν Παρθενῶνα.

3   The relative pronoun

The relatives ὅς ἥ ὅ and ὅστις ἥτις ὅ τι are used with the future indicative to express purpose; negative μή. This is particularly the case where, in English, an infinitive of purpose follows directly after a noun.

> *They sent ambassadors to announce this to the king.*
> πρέσβεις ἔπεμψαν οἵτινες ταῦτα ἀγγελοῦσι τῷ βασιλεῖ.

• The future participle, of course, could also be used:

πρέσβεις ἔπεμψαν ταῦτα τῷ βασιλεῖ ἀγγελοῦντας.

When writing in Greek it is a mistake automatically to assume that ἵνα will be the best way to express purpose. Often one of the other two constructions will produce more fluent prose.

A fourth way to express purpose, though less common than the other three, is the infinitive with τοῦ, i.e. the genitive of the infinitive. This is found particularly with negative purposes.

The harbour was fortified so that the barbarians might not be able to attack it.

ἐτειχίσθη ὁ λιμὴν τοῦ μὴ τοὺς βαρβάρους προσβάλλειν δύνασθαι.

Exercises

A

1   I'm explaining all this to you that you may never be ignorant in the future.
2   The Athenians sent messengers to deceive the Spartans concerning the wall.
3   Priam went into the Greek camp in order to ask Achilles to give back Hector's body.
4   After seeing a snake, the king sent his sons to Delphi to consult the god.
5   We punish those who do wrong so that they may become better citizens.
6   We sent out scouts to discover the enemy's whereabouts.
7   These ships have arrived to bring food and wine for the citizens.
8   Penelope used to deceive the suitors so that it would never be necessary to abandon her marriage with Odysseus (= the marriage of Odysseus).

63

9   Close the doors at once, so that Alcibiades and his friends can't get in.

10   I deliberately didn't wake my wife, so that she might sleep for as long as possible.

B

1   In their hatred of the authorities (= hating the authorities) some nobles formed a conspiracy with the intention of destroying the state.

2   We have good laws, so that the citizens may not neglect the gods or wrong their neighbours.

3   The Athenian general sent out four scouts to find out what the Spartans were intending to do.

4   We have come to London to see the queen.

5   The Athenians put Socrates to death so that all might know that he had broken the laws.

6   If only we had stayed in Greece, so that we might never have suffered these terrible things.

7   We sent a herald to reveal to those in the city that I was present with a large part of the army.

8   The judge decided to go abroad in order not to have to entertain his mother-in-law.

9   Xerxes said that he would despatch a great army to destroy both the Athenians and their city.

10   My friend will soon arrive here so that we can celebrate his birthday with a splendid dinner (= dining splendidly).

C

Meanwhile Cicero and his brother were staying in his villa near Tusculum. Learning that he himself had now been proscribed[1] by the authorities, he resolved to go to Astura, where he had a seaside[2] villa, so that from there he might sail to Macedonia. But when he had arrived there and was already putting out to sea, a flock of crows[3] flew up and began to settle on the boat, screeching and flapping[4] their wings. This was seen by everyone as an evil omen, and Cicero accordingly returned to shore.

On the same day Herennius and Popillius, sent by Antony to murder Cicero, also arrived at Astura. First of all they searched for him in his villa, but then, not finding him, they followed him down to the sea, where by now his slaves were carrying their master, still hoping to be able to make an escape. When therefore Cicero saw his assassins approaching, he ordered his slaves to set down the litter and, stretching out his neck, said, 'I shall die, then, in the fatherland which I often saved.' When they had killed him, his murderers chopped off his head and hands, brought them to Rome, and swiftly despatched a slave to report to Antony that his opponent was no more.

[1] I proscribe (i.e. I outlaw) = προγράφω.

[2] seaside (as an adjective) = παραθαλάσσιος -α -ον.

[3] a flock of crows = many crows.

[4] flapping: use κινέω.

Chapter 15: Result clauses

Consider the following sentences. In each the subordinate clause, introduced by *that* or *as to*, contains a result of what we are told in the main clause. These are known as result (or consecutive) clauses.

> He is *so* fat <u>that</u> he cannot get through the door.
>
> She was *such* a good woman <u>that</u> everyone admired her.
>
> I am not *so* foolish <u>as to</u> think Greek an easy language.

Each sentence also has a word (here italicised) which indicates that a result clause is coming. In Greek the main 'signpost' words are:

οὕτως (οὕτω before a consonant)	so (*with adjectives and adverbs*), in such a way
τοσοῦτος τοσαύτη τοσοῦτο	so great, so much
τοσοῦτοι τοσαῦται τοσαῦτα	so many
τοιοῦτος τοιαύτη τοιοῦτο	of such a kind, such
ἐς τοσοῦτο	to such an extent, so (*with verbs*)

Result clauses are expressed by two constructions in Greek.

1   The infinitive construction

ὥστε (*that, so that, as*), or sometimes ὡς, with the infinitive expresses a result which is a natural or likely consequence of the action or circumstances of the main verb.

• The subject of the infinitive is in the accusative if different from that of the main verb.

• It is either omitted or in the nominative if it is the same as the subject of the main verb.

• The negative is μή.

66

The teacher is so wise that everyone respects him.
ὁ διδάσκαλος οὕτω σοφός ἐστιν ὥστε πάντας αὐτὸν τιμᾶν.

The woman is so beautiful that she always has many admirers.
οὕτω καλή ἐστιν ἡ γυνὴ ὥστε ἀεὶ πολλοὺς ἔχειν μνηστῆρας.

Surely the boy isn't so stupid as to do this?
μῶν ὁ παῖς οὕτω μῶρός ἐστιν ὥστε τοῦτο ποιῆσαι;

2   The indicative construction

When the actual occurrence of the result is stressed, ὥστε is followed by the indicative. The negative is οὐ.

Alcestis loved her husband so much that she (actually) died on his behalf.
ἐς τοσοῦτο ἐφίλει ἡ Ἄλκηστις τὸν ἄνδρα ὥστε ὑπὲρ αὐτοῦ ἀπέθανεν.

It is very important to note that in practice the distinction between these two constructions is regularly blurred. When translating into Greek, it will often be possible to use either of them, the difference being simply a shift of emphasis.

The Athenians were so brave that they didn't fear the Spartans.
οἱ Ἀθηναῖοι οὕτως ἀνδρεῖοι ἦσαν ὥστε μὴ φοβεῖσθαι τοὺς Λακεδαιμονίους.

οἱ Ἀθηναῖοι οὕτως ἀνδρεῖοι ἦσαν ὥστε οὐκ ἐφοβοῦντο τοὺς Λακεδαιμονίους.

The first Greek version above suggests that the *natural consequence* of the Athenians' bravery was that they were unafraid of the Spartans. In the second version we are told that on a given occasion some Athenians were so brave that they *actually* didn't fear the Spartans.

ὥστε sometimes comes at the beginning of a sentence, or after a colon, used simply as a connecting word meaning *consequently, as a result.*

> *The Persians used to lead many strange wild beasts into battle; in consequence even the bravest of the enemy often used to flee.*
> οἱ Πέρσαι θήρια ἦγον εἰς μάχην πολλὰ καὶ δεινά· ὥστε τῶν πολεμίων καὶ οἱ ἀνδρειότατοι πολλάκις ἔφευγον.

A comparative adjective followed by ἢ ὥστε represents the English *too.*

> *The athlete was too strong to be beaten by his opponent.*
> ὁ ἀθλήτης ἰσχυρότερος ἦν ἢ ὥστε νικᾶσθαι ὑπὸ τοῦ ἐναντίου.

ἐφ' ᾧ and ἐφ' ᾧτε are used with either the infinitive or the future indicative to mean *on the condition that.* In either case the negative is μή.

> *They came to terms on the condition that the enemy should immediately depart from Attica.*
> συνέβησαν ἐφ' ᾧτε τοὺς πολεμίους εὐθὺς ἐξιέναι ἐκ τῆς Ἀττικῆς.
> or συνέβησαν ἐφ' ᾧτε οἱ πολέμιοι εὐθὺς ἐξίασιν ἐκ τῆς Ἀττικῆς.

Exercises

A

1   The Athenian orators are so clever that they always persuade their audiences.

2   So many were the barbarians that the Greeks were compelled to withdraw from the battlefield.

3   All my pupils are too lazy to learn this language accurately.

4   No one is so foolish as not to know that the women of Greece are very beautiful.

5   These young men are not strong enough to drag the ships down into the sea.

6   The king concealed himself very cleverly in the tree; as a result the soldiers did not see him sitting up there above their heads.

7   There are so many flowers in the garden that no one is able to gather them all.

8   The children were raising such a din that they did not hear the teacher's words.

9   During the summer the sun is so hot that no one works in the fields.

10   We shall allow you to stay with us on condition that you no longer attempt to betray the city to our enemies.

B   (result clauses and revision)

1   He said that the river was so deep that the travellers couldn't find a ford.

2   Such are the walls of our city that all enemies take to flight immediately they have seen them (= having seen them).

3   I promised to buy a dog to guard my mother's house at night.

4   The exiles were willing to return to Athens on condition that their children would be educated at public expense.

5   The builder is so ignorant that he is proposing to destroy some very famous handicraft.

6   Let us all hope that our leader will soon put a stop to this uproar.

7   The king's bodyguard were too brave to fear death.

8   Everyone wanted to know why so many teachers were so unhappy.

9   There are so many books in this school that no one can read them all.

10   Fifty soldiers were able to capture the enemy city, but were too few to keep a hold of it.

C

When both of us had eaten and drunk, the woman asked if I had enjoyed my meal[1]; for she said that she would be glad to find out[2]. For my part I praised her bread, but said that I couldn't drink the wine; for it was so sweet[3] that it could please no one. She however said that the wine came from Cyprus and was very famous, and on hearing this, I tasted it again; but it still seemed to me too sweet to be drunk with any pleasure. After a little pause, looking at the woman, 'So then[4],' I said, 'who are you, and where do you come from?' 'Well[5], I am an Egyptian,' she said, 'born in Greece, but very patriotic nonetheless.' And she proceeded to explain[6] to me how, after taking over her father's business in her native land, she had greatly increased his estate. For she said that she was wonderfully fond of money, and thought that only the very rich were truly happy. And I, hearing this, made no reply; for, a poor man myself, I found her words even more unpalatable than her wine.

[1] if I had enjoyed my meal = if the meal had pleased (use ἀρέσκω) me.

[2] that she would be glad to find out = that she would find out gladly.

[3] for it was so sweet etc.: note that this is still part of the indirect speech. The accusative and infinitive construction continues after the semicolon, without any negative sense, despite οὐκ ἔφην earlier.

[4] This question can usefully be started with Σὺ τοίνυν.

[5] Well (at the beginning of a reply): use ἀλλά.

[6] she proceeded to explain = going on (προϊοῦσα) she explained.

Chapter 16: Conditional sentences

Conditional sentences fall into two main groups, one of so-called **open** conditions, and a second of **unreal** conditions, sometimes called **unfulfilled** (present and past) and **remote** (future). Open conditions deal with actual facts, unreal conditions with hypothetical or unlikely sets of circumstances, signalled in English, generally, by the words *would* or *should*.

Each group is further subdivided into three time zones, present, past and future. In all, therefore, there are six basic types of conditional sentence. At the outset, before looking at the rules for the Greek construction at all, it is essential to grasp the distinction between these six types in English: in the case of conditionals, inaccurate translation into Greek is as often the result of failure to analyse the English correctly as it is of ignorance of the Greek construction.

Open

<u>Present</u>:	If they are doing this, they are doing wrong.
<u>Past</u>:	If they did/were doing this, they did/were doing wrong.
<u>Future</u>:	If they do this, they will do wrong.

Unreal

<u>Present</u>:	If they were doing this, they would be doing wrong.
<u>Past</u>:	If they had done this, they would have done wrong.
<u>Future</u>:	If they were to do this, they would do wrong.

In Greek conditional sentences, we refer to the *if* clause as the **protasis**, and to the main clause as the **apodosis**.

• The words for *if* are εἰ and ἐάν; *even if* is καὶ εἰ or καὶ ἐάν.

• The negative in the protasis is μή, in the apodosis οὐ, unless the clause has its own reasons for using μή.

Alternative conditions (*whether ... or*) are introduced by εἴτε ... εἴτε.

But if not or *otherwise* is εἰ δὲ μή, even if ἐάν precedes.
> *If you come here, you will receive gifts; if not, you will be punished.*
> ἐὰν δεῦρο ἔλθῃς, δῶρα δέξῃ· εἰ δὲ μή, κολασθήσῃ.

Open Conditions

<u>Present and Past</u>

εἰ with the indicative in the protasis, and indicative in the apodosis; tense as English.

> *If they are doing this, they are doing wrong.*
> εἰ τοῦτο ποιοῦσιν, ἁμαρτάνουσιν.

> *If they were doing this, they were doing wrong.*
> εἰ τοῦτο ἐποίουν, ἡμάρτανον.

> *If they did this, they did wrong.*
> εἰ τοῦτο ἐποίησαν, ἥμαρτον.

<u>Future</u>

ἐάν with the subjunctive (present or aorist) in the protasis, future indicative in the apodosis.

> *If they do this, they will do wrong.*
> ἐὰν τοῦτο ποιῶσιν, ἁμαρτήσονται.

ἐάν is really εἰ + ἄν; ἤν and ἄν are sometimes found instead.

εἰ with the future indicative is also found instead of ἐάν with the subjunctive, usually in threats or warnings.

Note that in the protasis of a future open condition in English we use the present tense to refer to the future. This is known as a 'hidden' or 'concealed' future. It is important not to be misled by this.

Unreal Conditions

<u>Present</u>

εἰ with the imperfect indicative in the protasis; imperfect indicative with ἄν in the apodosis.

> *If they were doing this (now), they would be doing wrong.*
> εἰ τοῦτο ἐποίουν, ἡμάρτανον ἄν.

<u>Past</u>

εἰ with the aorist indicative in the protasis; aorist indicative with ἄν in the apodosis.

> *If they had done this, they would have done wrong.*
> εἰ τοῦτο ἐποίησαν, ἥμαρτον ἄν.

<u>Future</u>

εἰ with the optative (present or aorist) in the protasis; optative with ἄν in the apodosis.

> *If they were to do this, they would do wrong.*
> εἰ τοῦτο ποιοῖεν, ἁμαρτάνοιεν ἄν.

The particle ἄν can't come first word in a sentence or clause; it often comes either before or after the verb, but can also be attached to negatives and interrogatives, or to any emphatic word.

The two halves of a conditional sentence may refer to different times. Greek simply uses the construction appropriate to each clause.

If you had read the book, you would not be at a loss.
εἰ ἀνέγνως τὴν βίβλον, οὐκ ἂν ἠπόρεις.

The imperfect indicative, as well as referring to the present, may be used also to refer to a continuous or repeated act in the past. Context will usually make it clear which of the two possible meanings is intended.

If they had been doing this, they would have been doing wrong.
εἰ τοῦτο ἐποίουν, ἡμάρτανον ἄν.

In an unreal future condition *if they were to do this* might, in English, appear as *if they did this*. The whole sentence needs to be looked at to avoid confusion with an open past condition.

For indefinite conditional clauses see Chapter 19.

Conditional sentences in indirect speech

Protasis

The normal rules for subordinate clauses in indirect speech apply (see Chapter 13), i.e. if the main verb is primary, the verb in the protasis is unchanged. If the main verb is historic, either the mood and tense remain unchanged, or the original tense is retained but the mood becomes optative. The historic tenses of the indicative should not be changed to the optative; and if an original subjunctive is so changed, εἰ must replace ἐάν.

Apodosis

If the ὅτι/ὡς construction is used, the normal rules for that construction apply (see Chapter 11). If the infinitive or participle construction is used, the infinitive or participle will be in the same tense as the indicative or optative of the direct speech, the present infinitive and participle also doing duty for the imperfect. In all cases, if ἄν would have been used in the direct speech, it must remain.

There follow, worked in full, two examples, a) of an open future condition, and b) of an unreal past condition. These should be studied carefully.

a)   *If they do this, they will do wrong.*
       ἐὰν τοῦτο ποιῶσιν, ἁμαρτήσονται.

      He says that if they do this, they will do wrong.
       λέγει ὅτι, ἐὰν τοῦτο ποιῶσιν, ἁμαρτήσονται.
       φησὶν αὐτούς, ἐὰν τοῦτο ποιῶσιν, ἁμαρτήσεσθαι.

      He knows that if they do this, they will do wrong.
       οἶδεν αὐτούς, ἐὰν τοῦτο ποιῶσιν, ἁμαρτησομένους.

      He said that if they did this, they would do wrong.
       εἶπεν ὅτι, ἐὰν τοῦτο ποιῶσιν, ἁμαρτήσονται (ἁμαρτήσοιντο).
                   εἰ τοῦτο ποιοῖεν,

       ἔφη αὐτούς, ἐὰν τοῦτο ποιῶσιν, ἁμαρτήσεσθαι.
                   εἰ τοῦτο ποιοῖεν,

      He knew that if they did this, they would do wrong.
       ᾔδει αὐτούς, ἐὰν τοῦτο ποιῶσιν, ἁμαρτησομένους.
                   εἰ τοῦτο ποιοῖεν,

b)   *If they had done this, they would have done wrong.*
       εἰ τοῦτο ἐποίησαν, ἥμαρτον ἄν.

      He says that if they had done this, they would have done wrong.
       λέγει ὅτι, εἰ τοῦτο ἐποίησαν, ἥμαρτον ἄν.
       φησὶν αὐτούς, εἰ τοῦτο ἐποίησαν, ἁμαρτεῖν ἄν.

      He knows that if they had done this, they would have done wrong.
       οἶδεν αὐτούς, εἰ τοῦτο ἐποίησαν, ἁμαρτόντας ἄν.

      He said that if they had done this, they would have done wrong.
       εἶπεν ὅτι, εἰ τοῦτο ἐποίησαν, ἥμαρτον ἄν.
       ἔφη αὐτούς, εἰ τοῦτο ἐποίησαν, ἁμαρτεῖν ἄν.

      He knew that if they had done this, they would have done wrong.
       ᾔδει αὐτούς, εἰ τοῦτο ἐποίησαν, ἁμαρτόντας ἄν.

Potential sentences

Direct statements in English are often modified by the auxiliaries *may,
might, could, would* etc. We refer to this usage as **potential.**

In Greek the optative (present or aorist) with ἄν is used to refer to present or
future time, the imperfect and aorist indicative, again with ἄν, to refer to the
past. These usages are similar to conditional apodoses, but it should be noted
that the imperfect indicative with ἄν referring to present time is uncommon
in the potential sense.

It would be silly to do this.	μῶρον ἂν εἴη τοῦτο ποιεῖν.
I should like to see the king.	βουλοίμην ἂν ἰδεῖν τὸν βασιλέα.
You might have believed.	ἐπιστεύσατε ἄν.

Exercises

A

1   If you come at once, you will see a very famous poet in the street.
2   If the boy had not thrown the stones, he would not have been punished
    by his father.
3   If they said that my brother is a fool, they were certainly mistaken.
4   Even if you were to set out at once, girls, you would not arrive at
    Delphi in three days.
5   If I were richer than Croesus, I would be giving a lot of money to the
    poor.
6   If you think it is easy to learn the Greek language, you are even more
    ignorant than I thought before.
7   If the young men stole the judge's money, they will soon be arrested
    and punished.
8   We would all be very happy, if our parents were still alive.

9   If the soldiers had not guarded the gates, Philip would easily have
     taken our camp.
10   If you were to open the door, you would see my friends waiting there.

B

1   Unless he hurries, he will find no one still at home.
2   If I had not spent all the money which you gave me, I should now be
     very rich.
3   If you thought that the farmer was angry with his slaves, you were
     making a big mistake.
4   If the thief had not seen that the door was already open, he would
     never have been able to enter the teacher's house.
5   Unless you depart from here immediately, I shall send for a policeman
     to arrest you and take you off to prison.
6   If the messenger does not come tomorrow, we shall have to leave the
     city and search for him.
7   If you do what is necessary, all will be well; if not, many people will
     die in vain.
8   If you were to ask my daughter why she doesn't have a husband, she
     would quickly reply that it is none of your business (= that it doesn't
     at all concern you).
9   If my brother has arrived at last, ask him where his friends are.
10   Our ancestors would never have wanted to send men to the moon.

C   (including conditions in indirect speech)

1   How many soldiers would die in battle, if Xerxes were to lead out his
     army at once?
2   If our bankers were not so greedy for gain, there wouldn't now be
     such a financial crisis (= we shouldn't now be so short of money).
3   The teacher said that the students would be very severely punished if
     they did not read the poems of Homer.
4   You are slandering the Thebans, Athenians, if you accuse them of
     cowardice.

5   If I were to kill the priest of Zeus, I should rightly be called impious.

6   If I hadn't drunk so much wine, I shouldn't be ill today.

7   The general said that if the reinforcements had come, he would have saved both the city and many citizens.

8   If a storm were arising, we should not be able to sail out of the harbour.

9   Unless you leave the city at once, everyone will know that you are the murderer of your brother's wife.

10   The old man said that if his daughter were to be ill, he would send for the doctor at once.

D

After the murder of Agamemnon, his son, a lad named Orestes, would certainly also have been put to death, had he not been saved by his sister. For Electra, realising that he was in great danger, secretly sent the boy away to the court of [1] Strophius, his uncle and king of the Phocians; and there Orestes was brought up well with the king's son, Pylades, who quickly became his most steadfast friend. Electra frequently reminded her brother by messengers of the necessity to take vengeance on his father's murderers: 'For', she said, 'if you return to Argos and kill Clytemnestra and Aegisthus, you will not only act justly, but will also deliver the state and all its citizens; but if you don't do this, no one will any longer believe that you are a true son of your father Agamemnon.' When he had grown to man's estate[2], Orestes set out for Delphi in order to ask the god what would happen, if he were to kill his mother. Persuaded then by the Pythia, he secretly came to Argos, pretending to have come from Strophius with the news that Orestes was dead; and after visiting his father's tomb and making himself known to his sister, not long afterwards he slaughtered Clytemnestra, and along with her Aegisthus.

[1] to the court of = παρά with accusative.

[2] When he had grown to man's estate = Having become a man: use ἀνὴρ γίγνεσθαι.

Chapter 17: Participles II

Some information on participles and their use has already been given in previous chapters. The following details make the picture more complete.

1   Causal

a) ἅτε, οἷον and οἷα δή, *inasmuch as, seeing that, since,* are used with a participle to express a cause which is presented as a fact.

> *Since he was a general, the enemy did not put him to death.*
> οὐκ ἀπέκτειναν αὐτὸν οἱ πολέμιοι ἅτε στρατηγὸν ὄντα.

> *Seeing that they were few in number, the Spartans decided to retreat.*
> τοῖς Λακεδαιμονίοις οἷα δὴ ὀλίγοις οὖσιν ἔδοξεν ἀναχωρῆσαι.

b) ὡς, *on the grounds that,* with a participle expresses an alleged reason, i.e. a reason given not as a definite fact, but as something said or felt to be the case.

> *The Athenians blamed their general for having accepted bribes.*
> = *The Athenians blamed their general on the grounds that he had accepted bribes.*
> οἱ Ἀθηναῖοι ἐν αἰτίᾳ εἶχον τὸν στρατηγὸν ὡς δῶρα λαβόντα.

With both the above uses the negative is οὐ.

2   Concessive

a) καίπερ with a participle (negative οὐ) means *although.* Care needs to be taken with the arrangement of words so as to avoid beginning a sentence with καίπερ.

> *Although he was ill, they appointed Nicias general.*
> τὸν Νικίαν καίπερ νοσοῦντα στρατηγὸν κατέστησαν.

b) καὶ ταῦτα with a participle expresses the meaning *and that too though.*

They executed the men, and that too though they knew they were guiltless.
ἀπέκτειναν τοὺς ἄνδρας, καὶ ταῦτα εἰδότες αὐτοὺς ἀναιτίους ὄντας.

3 Comparative

ὥσπερ with a participle expresses *as if*; negative οὐ.

> *I loved him as if he were a brother.*
> ἐφίλουν αὐτὸν ὥσπερ ἀδελφὸν ὄντα.

It is important to distinguish this use of ὥσπερ from its use with an indicative verb, when it means *exactly as, just as.*
> *The doctor came, just as he had promised.*
> ὁ ἰατρὸς ἦλθεν, ὥσπερ ὑπέσχετο.

4 Conditional

A participial phrase may take the place of the protasis of a conditional sentence. When a participle is used like this, the negative is μή, as it would have been in a conditional clause.

> *If you do this, you will find your children.*
> ταῦτα ποιήσας εὑρήσεις τοὺς παῖδας.

> *Unless you do this, you will never find your children.*
> ταῦτα μὴ ποιήσας οὐδέποτε εὑρήσεις τοὺς παῖδας.

5 Meaning *with*

The following participles may be used as equivalents of the English word *with*.

ἔχων	having	ἄγων	leading, bringing
φέρων	carrying, bringing	λαβών	having taken

> *He arrived in the camp with many soldiers.*
> ἀφίκετο εἰς τὸ στρατόπεδον πολλοὺς ἔχων στρατιώτας.

6 After certain verbs

Many verbs use participles in their normal construction. The following are some of the most common of them:

τυγχάνω	I happen	*He happened to have departed.* ἀπελθὼν ἔτυχεν.
διατελέω	I continue	*They continued to fight for three days.* τρεῖς ἡμέρας μαχόμενοι διετέλεσαν.
ἀνέχομαι	I endure, bear	*They couldn't bear to hear this.* οὐκ ἠνείχοντο ταῦτα ἀκούοντες.
παύομαι λήγω	I cease, stop I cease, stop	*They stopped fighting immediately.* εὐθὺς ἐπαύσαντο μαχόμενοι.
χαίρω ἥδομαι τέρπομαι	I am glad, enjoy I enjoy, am pleased I enjoy, take pleasure	*I was glad to see the boy.* ἔχαιρον ὁρῶν τὸν παῖδα.
ὀργίζομαι ἀγανακτέω ἄχθομαι	I am angry I am displeased I am cross, annoyed	*I am cross to learn this.* ἄχθομαι ταῦτα μανθάνων
ἄρχομαι	I begin (by)	*I shall begin by saying this, that ...* ἄρξομαι τοῦτο λέγων, ὅτι ...

ἄρχομαι with the infinitive = I begin to ...

φαίνομαι	I am obviously	*He was obviously wise.* ἐφαίνετο σοφὸς ὤν.

φανερός εἰμι and δῆλός εἰμι (both = *I am clearly*) are used in the same way as φαίνομαι: *He clearly wanted this.*
φανερὸς ἦν ταῦτα βουλόμενος.

φαίνομαι with the infinitive = *I appear to be (but may not be).*
He appeared to be wise.
ἐφαίνετο σοφὸς εἶναι.

λανθάνω	I escape the notice of	*He left without us seeing him.* = *He escaped our notice having left.* ἔλαθεν ἡμᾶς ἀπελθών.

φθάνω   I anticipate, get   *He arrived before us.*
          in before (someone)   = *He anticipated us having arrived.*
                                   ἔφθασεν ἡμᾶς ἀφικόμενος.

With both λανθάνω and φθάνω the construction may be inverted.
     He left without us seeing him.   *He arrived before us.*
     ἀπῆλθε λαθὼν ἡμᾶς.   ἀφίκετο φθάσας ἡμᾶς.

Exercises

A

1   We do not wish to use these ships as they are old and in bad condition.
2   The beggar came into our village with nothing; but because he was my father's friend, I gave him money and clothes.
3   Although they had suffered terrible things in the war, the Athenians refused to give in.
4   The prisoners were put to death on the grounds that they had plotted against those in authority.
5   The fugitives escaped from the city unobserved by those guarding the gates.
6   'We shall continue fighting for a long time,' said the general, 'and will never surrender our city.'
7   Stop throwing stones at the swans, you wretch; for they are sacrosanct in that they belong to the queen.
8   It was clear to everyone that the orator was trying to deceive the citizens.
9   The Athenians condemned Socrates to death although he had done no wrong.
10   All the students were pleased to hear that the teacher was ill.

B

1   He happened to have heard Demosthenes speaking in the assembly.
2   The Athenian ships were the first to arrive in the harbour.

3   If we do not rebuild the long walls, we shall never be able to resist the Spartans.

4   Although he scorned the gods, the king sent his son to Delphi with an offering for Apollo.

5   These natives don't seem to be well disposed towards us; but I don't know if we can escape without being seen.

6   Xenophon resolved to advance with great caution, although the Armenians had already abandoned their cities and fled into the mountains.

7   When the allies had arrived, the general came forward and began by praising the courage of all his soldiers.

8   The deserters were clearly unwilling to return home, as if they already knew what the Athenians were intending.

9   The ephors recalled Pausanias on the grounds that he wanted to go over to the Persians.

10   The young man put out to sea at dawn since he wanted to get to the island before his friends.

C   (revision of all constructions using participles)

1   Those who enslave their neighbours are never praised by the wise.

2   I am not at all pleased to hear that representatives of the Corinthians have been invited here; for they didn't come to our aid during the Persian invasion of Attica.

3   Sending for her sons, the queen said that she knew that they were plotting against their father.

4   Although he pretends to be very wise, in reality our teacher knows absolutely nothing.

5   Now that the ambassadors are present, everyone knows that the Thebans will never come to help us.

6   Our allies must flee away, soldiers, and board their ships without being seen.

7   In great despair the king sent messengers to ask the Pythia why he had lost all his wealth.

8   Quite clearly you have already heard of the death of my friend's mother.

9   Having seen that the sun was already rising, the priests went into the temple to pray to the god.

10   My neighbour happened to be away from home because his father was seriously ill.

D

After the battle, when Nicias was on the point of leading the Athenians away, Gylippus saw that the Syracusans were already drinking wine after their victory, and knew that he could neither compel nor persuade them to abandon their festivities and attack the Athenians as they withdrew. But Hermocrates on his own initiative[1] devised a scheme as follows to deceive Nicias. He sent some trusted friends, who claimed that they had come from those in the city with whom Nicias had often been in secret communication[2], and warned him not to set out during the coming[3] night, as the Syracusans were already guarding the passes and had set ambushes for him. Completely taken in by their report, Nicias, though he wished to get away as quickly as possible, decided to wait, with the result that his worst fears were quickly realised[4]. For the next day the enemy were on the march before him, seized the passes, destroyed the bridges and sent out a large detachment of cavalry to oppose the Athenians at every stage as they retreated.

[1] on his own initiative = ἀφ' ἑαυτοῦ.

[2] had... been in secret communication with: use κρυφαίους λόγους ποιεῖσθαι πρός with accusative.

[3] coming: use ἐπιγιγνόμενος -η -ον here (= ensuing).

[4] his worst fears were ... realised = what he most feared happened.

Chapter 18: Verbs of fearing, precaution and preventing

Verbs of fearing

1   Fears for the **future**

These are expressed by μή followed by the subjunctive in primary sequence and by the optative in historic sequence. By the so-called 'vivid' construction the subjunctive may also be used in historic sequence.

• The present subjunctive and optative are used for continuous or repeated action, the aorist for individual or single action.

• The negative is μὴ οὐ.

• The normal verbs of fearing are φοβέομαι and δέδοικα. Note too that the phrases φόβος ἐστί (*there is a fear, people are afraid*) and κίνδυνός ἐστι (*there is a danger*) are used with the same construction.

> *I am afraid that my friend will make a mistake.*
> φοβοῦμαι μὴ ὁ φίλος ἁμάρτῃ.
>
> *I was afraid that my mother would not arrive in time.*
> ἐφοβούμην μὴ ἡ μήτηρ οὐ καιρίως ἀφίκοιτο (or ἀφίκηται).

2   Fears for the **present** and **past**

These too are introduced by μή (negative μὴ οὐ).

• The verb is in the appropriate tense of the indicative.

> *I am afraid that this is true.*
> φοβοῦμαι μὴ τοῦτο ἀληθές ἐστιν.

I was afraid that my brother had fallen down.
ἐφοβούμην μὴ κατέπεσεν ὁ ἀδελφός μου.

3   With an **infinitive**:

When a verb of fearing is followed by an infinitive in English, Greek uses the infinitive as well.

I am afraid to go into the house.
φοβοῦμαι εἰσελθεῖν εἰς τὴν οἰκίαν.

The verb κινδυνεύω (*I am in danger, run a risk*) also takes an infinitive.
He is in danger of being killed. = He is likely to be killed.
κινδυνεύει ἀποθανεῖν.

Verbs of precaution

These are regularly followed by ὅπως (negative ὅπως μή) with the future indicative. In historic sequence the future indicative usually remains unchanged, though the future optative is occasionally found.

• The most common verbs in question are:

ὁράω	I see to it
σκοπέω/-έομαι	I see to it
σκεπτέον ἐστί	it must be seen to
εὐλαβέομαι	I take care
ἐπιμελέομαι	I take care
φυλάττομαι	I am on my guard
φροντίζω	I take heed

See to it that you always help your friends.
σκόπει ὅπως ἀεὶ ὠφελήσεις τοὺς φίλους.

They took care that the enemy should not do this.
ηὐλαβοῦντο ὅπως μὴ οἱ πολέμιοι τοῦτο ποιήσουσιν.

The present or aorist subjunctive and optative, as in purpose clauses, are sometimes found instead of the future indicative.

Be on your guard that you don't fall into danger.
φυλάττου ὅπως μὴ εἰς κίνδυνον πέσῃς.

μή or μὴ οὐ with the subjunctive or optative (without ὅπως) are sometimes found in negative clauses after verbs of precaution.

See to it that we don't suffer.
ὁρᾶτε μὴ πάθωμεν.

If the verb of precaution is a second-person imperative, it is regularly omitted, giving a strong sense of urgency to the instruction.

See that you do this.
ὅπως τοῦτο ποιήσεις.

Verbs of preventing, hindering, forbidding and denying

κωλύω	I hinder, prevent
εἴργω	I hinder, prevent
ἐμποδών εἰμι with dative	I hinder, prevent
ἀπαγορεύω with dative	I forbid
ἀπεῖπον with dative	I forbade
οὐκ ἐάω	I do not allow, forbid
(ἀπ)αρνέομαι	I deny

These verbs of preventing, hindering, forbidding and denying are regularly followed by the infinitive preceded by a redundant μή.

I am preventing the soldier from killing the child.
εἴργω τὸν στρατιώτην μὴ ἀποκτεῖναι τὸν παῖδα.

87

The judge forbade his daughter to converse with strangers.
ὁ κριτὴς ἀπεῖπε τῇ θυγατρὶ μὴ διαλέγεσθαι τοῖς ξένοις.

• If the verb of preventing is itself negative, or is a question expecting the answer no, μὴ οὐ is used with the infinitive.

I'm not preventing you from leaving.
οὐκ εἴργω ὑμᾶς μὴ οὐκ ἀπελθεῖν.

• κωλύω, even when negative itself, usually takes just the simple infinitive.

κωλύω τὸν στρατιώτην ἀποκτεῖναι τὸν παῖδα.
οὐ κωλύω ὑμᾶς ἀπελθεῖν.

• Both present and aorist infinitives are used, but with verbs of denying the aorist has a definite past meaning.

I didn't deny having made a mistake.
οὐκ ἀπηρνήθην μὴ οὐχ ἁμαρτεῖν.

τὸ μή (or just τό) and τὸ μὴ οὐ are also found with the infinitive.
He prevents them from doing this.
εἴργει αὐτοὺς τὸ [μὴ] τοῦτο ποιεῖν.

He doesn't prevent them from doing this.
οὐκ εἴργει αὐτοὺς τὸ μὴ οὐ τοῦτο ποιεῖν.

Similarly τοῦ μή (or less frequently just τοῦ); but virtually never τοῦ μὴ οὐ.
He prevents them from doing this.
εἴργει αὐτοὺς τοῦ [μὴ] τοῦτο ποιεῖν.

Exercises

A

1   I am afraid that you are all talking nonsense.
2   Take care, citizens, always to honour both the gods and your ancestors.
3   Do not be afraid to punish those who betrayed our country to the barbarians.
4   The Spartans did not prevent the Athenians from rebuilding the long walls.
5   The children were afraid that their parents would find out what had happened.
6   There is a great danger that our scouts won't be able to get back to the camp.
7   With a huge shout the captain forbade the sailors to leave the ship.
8   The girls were taking care not to annoy their grandfather while playing in the garden.
9   He was afraid that his friends had lost their way on their journey.
10   No one will prevent him from running twenty stades every day.

B

1   I am not afraid to say that Philip is an evil man, worthy of all kinds of punishments.
2   Unless you want to lose many soldiers, you will take care that you are never at a loss for provisions while on the march.
3   The citizens were afraid that the guards had been bribed to open the city gates.
4   The Armenians wanted to prevent Xenophon from crossing the river.
5   Honourable men are never afraid to speak the truth.
6   I was very much afraid that, since he was ugly, my son would never find a beautiful wife.

7   Gentlemen are always on their guard not to do anything unworthy of
      their reputation

8   People are afraid that the sun will soon become so hot as to destroy
      the whole world.

9   No one denies that the Corcyraeans are trying to the best of their
      ability to become good citizens.

10   I am afraid that my friends spent a very great deal of money in vain in
      their attempt to have their son taught music.

C

The commander-in-chief, perceiving that the soldiers were disaffected[1], and
fearing that, unless he found some means of appeasing them[2], they would no
longer be obedient, called everyone together and spoke as follows. 'It would
be foolish, men, to deny that, lacking provisions as we do, we are in great
difficulties. We must remember this, however, that had we not been
unexpectedly prevented from going forward, we would by now have
overtaken the enemy. If only they had waited and had been prepared to
fight! As it is, if they have continued their march, they must by this time
have reached the mountains, where it would be difficult for us to pursue
them; and, even if they join battle with us of their own accord[3], they will
have the hill tribes on their side[4]. So, you must see to it that at all times you
obey your commanders, so that we may in the end be victorious and return
home to our wives and children.'

[1] disaffected: use δυσχεραίνω.

[2] unless he found some means of appeasing then = unless in some way he
    might appease (καταπραΰνω) them.

[3] of their own accord: use ἑκών in agreement with the subject.

[4] on their side = (as) allies.

Chapter 19: Indefinites

> He did what he wanted.
> He did whatever he wanted.

The first of the two sentences above expresses something **definite**, the second something general or **indefinite**.

English usually achieves this indefinite sense by adding -*ever* to the pronoun, adverb or conjunction in question (*whatever, however, whenever* etc); Greek uses the subjunctive with ἄν in primary sequence, the optative without ἄν in historic sequence. The negative is always μή.

• For pronouns etc. use the indefinite relative forms, as in indirect questions (ὅστις, ὅπου etc.).

• ὁπότε, ὅτε and ἐπειδή coalesce with ἄν to produce ὁπόταν, ὅταν and ἐπειδάν.

• The general nature of indefinite clauses means that the subjunctive and optative are very often present tense; but the aorist is also found.

> *He always says whatever he wants.*
> ἀεὶ λέγει ὅ τι ἂν βούληται.

> *He always used to say whatever he wanted.*
> ἀεὶ ἔλεγεν ὅ τι βούλοιτο.

When the words for *if* (ἐάν in primary sequence and εἰ in historic) introduce indefinite conditional clauses, the indefinite forms of the relevant pronouns etc. should be used (τις, που, ποτε etc.).
> *If ever I drink red wine, I have a headache the next day.*
> ἐάν ποτε ἐρυθρὸν πίω οἶνον, τὴν κεφαλὴν ἀλγῶ τῇ ὑστεραίᾳ.

If ever anyone spoke intelligently in the assembly, the Athenians were delighted.

εἴ τις συνετῶς λέγοι ἐν τῇ ἐκκλησίᾳ, οἱ Ἀθηναῖοι ἔχαιρον.

Exercises

A

1 He used to give away to his friends whatever he didn't wish to keep.
2 Whatever kind of things the Persians say, I shall never believe them.
3 The Athenian general persuaded his troops to do whatever the allies wanted.
4 Whatever happens, we shall always remember this day.
5 Whenever he heard a cuckoo, he always knew that summer was not far away.
6 We shall all do whatever you want.
7 If ever he saw someone beating a child, my father used to get very angry indeed.
8 Wherever the girls happened to be, they always wrote letters to their friends.
9 Whenever I see my wife and children, I thank the gods who have given me so many blessings.
10 The captain ordered his men not to take the enemy alive, but to put to death at once however many they captured.

B (indefinites and revision)

1 However much money men have, they always want to acquire more.
2 All were willing to do whatever the captain ordered.
3 Stop shouting in the street, boys; for it is the middle of the night and I am trying to sleep.
4 If ever my sister drank wine to excess, she was always ill on the following day.
5 Wherever I go in Italy, I always find many friends.

6   Unless Nicias arrives soon with reinforcements, the enemy will conquer us and set up a trophy.

7   Do not be afraid of returning home; for nothing will stop your parents giving you a splendid welcome.

8   I urged you to say whatever you wanted to the Armenian king.

9   The ruler was so cruel that the citizens were afraid to say whatever they thought.

10   She shall have music wherever she goes.

C

Hard pressed by persistent enemy activity[1], the Dolonci at last sent envoys to Delphi to ask for the god's advice[2]; for they were well aware that they were in serious need of a brave and reliable leader. In reply to them the Pythia spoke as follows: 'You must ask whoever first invites you into his house after you have left here to be ruler of your country.' So the Dolonci set out from Delphi, with high hopes[3] that they would soon meet such a man. But, wherever they went in either Phocis or Boeotia[4], they found no one willing to offer such entertainment. So they decided to make their way to Athens.

Now there was in Athens at that time a certain rich man called Miltiades. One day as he sat on his verandah he saw the Doloncian envoys passing by, and noticing that their clothing was not at all local, he stood up and invited them into his house. And they, when they had gone in, revealed all the Pythia's instructions, and asked him to be their king. At first Miltiades was so astonished that he said nothing in reply; but later, he willingly accepted their proposals, thinking that in this way he would be able to leave behind both Athens and the tyranny of Pisistratus.

[1] by persistent enemy activity = the enemy always attacking (gen. abs.).

[2] to ask for the god's advice = to ask the god what they should do.

[3] with high hopes = very much hoping.

[4] in either Phocis or Boeotia: use genitive, i.e. of either Phocis or Boeotia.

Chapter 20: Temporal clauses

Temporal (time) clauses may relate to the present, the past or the future.

Present and Past

All temporal clauses referring to the present or past, unless they are indefinite, have their verbs in the indicative.

The conjunctions which regularly introduce them are:

<u>referring to the same time as the main verb</u>

ὅτε, ὁπότε, ἡνίκα	when, at the time when
ἕως, μέχρι, ὅσον (χρόνον)	as long as
ἕως, ἐν ᾧ	while

<u>referring to time before the main verb</u>

ἐπεί, ἐπειδή, ὡς	when, after
ἐπεὶ/ἐπειδὴ τάχιστα, ἐπεὶ πρῶτον	as soon as
ἐξ οὗ, ἀφ' οὗ	(ever) since, since the time when

While there is an opportunity, we are building the wall.
ἐν ᾧ καιρός ἐστιν, οἰκοδομοῦμεν τὸ τεῖχος.

When we were building the wall, the enemy were already approaching.
ὅτ' ᾠκοδομοῦμεν τὸ τεῖχος, οἱ πολέμιοι ἤδη προσεχώρουν.

As soon as the enemy had arrived, they destroyed the wall.
ἐπεὶ τάχιστα ἀφίκοντο οἱ πολέμιοι, τὸ τεῖχος διέφθειραν.

As in the third example above, the aorist is regularly used in temporal clauses to translate the English pluperfect.

Many temporal clauses can be more neatly translated by the use of a participle, either agreeing with a noun or pronoun in the main clause, or as part of a genitive absolute.

The second sentence above could well be:
    οἰκοδομούντων ἡμῶν τὸ τεῖχος, ἤδη προσεχώρουν οἱ πολεμιοι.
And the third:
    ἀφικόμενοι οἱ πολέμιοι διέφθειραν τὸ τεῖχος.

• Remember that indefinite temporal clauses use the indefinite construction (see Chapter 19).

> *Whenever the authorities come together, they always talk nonsense.*
> ὁπόταν συνέλθωσιν οἱ ἐν τέλει, ἀεὶ φλυαροῦσιν.

Even here a participle could replace the indefinite clause:
    συνελθόντες οἱ ἐν τέλει ἀεὶ φλυαροῦσιν.

Future

• Temporal clauses referring to the future use the indefinite construction.

> *When my father arrives, I shall tell him to leave at once.*
> ἐπειδὰν ἀφίκηται ὁ πατήρ μου, κελεύσω αὐτὸν εὐθὺς ἀπελθεῖν.

Until and *Before*

Temporal clauses introduced by the English words *until* and *before* are regularly those which cause the greatest difficulties.

Until

ἕως, μέχρι or μέχρι οὗ is used with the indicative in a clause where a fixed, definite or known time is referred to.

> *I waited until my friend arrived.*
> ἔμεινα ἕως ἀφίκετο ὁ φίλος μου.

• When *until* refers to a time which is not fixed or known, the same conjunctions are used with the indefinite construction, i.e. with the subjunctive + ἄν in primary sequence, and the optative alone in historic.

> *Wait until the judge arrives.*
> μένετε ἕως ἂν ἀφίκηται ὁ κριτής.

> *They waited until the enemy should charge = for the enemy to charge.*
> ἔμενον ἕως ἐπίοιεν οἱ πολέμιοι.

• After a <u>negative</u> main verb, when *before* can be substituted for *until* with no alteration of meaning, πρίν is regularly used instead of the other conjunctions (though they also are found), with the same constructions.

> *I did not go away until/before my friend arrived.*
> οὐκ ἀπῆλθον πρὶν ἀφίκετο ὁ φίλος μου.

> *I shall not go away until/before my friend arrives.*
> οὐκ ἄπειμι πρὶν ἂν ἀφίκηται ὁ φίλος μου.

Before

After a <u>positive</u> main verb, when *until* cannot be substituted, πρίν takes the infinitive. The subject of the infinitive is in the accusative unless it is the same as the subject of the main verb, in which case it is not expressed, any complement of the infinitive appearing in the nominative.

The citizens departed before the barbarians arrived in the city.
οἱ πολῖται ἀπῆλθον πρὶν τοὺς βαρβάρους ἀφικέσθαι εἰς τὴν πόλιν.

Before departing my father gave his sister many gifts.
πρὶν ἀπελθεῖν ὁ πατήρ μου ἔδωκε πολλὰ δῶρα τῇ ἀδελφῇ.

The soldier jumped into the trench before he became visible to the enemy.
ὁ στρατιώτης κατεπήδησεν εἰς τὴν τάφρον πρὶν φανερὸς γενέσθαι τοῖς πολεμίοις.

• After a <u>negative</u> main verb, when *until* can be substituted for *before*, πρίν is used, as above under *until*, with the indicative or the indefinite construction.

I did not go away before/until my friend arrived.
οὐκ ἀπῆλθον πρὶν ἀφίκετο ὁ φίλος μου.

I shall not go away before/until my friend arrives.
οὐκ ἄπειμι πρὶν ἂν ἀφίκηται ὁ φίλος μου.

πρότερον ἤ may be used in exactly the same way as πρίν.

πρότερον or πρόσθε(ν) may be used to look forward to a temporal clause with πρίν.

They didn't stop fighting until they had killed the enemy general.
οὐ πρότερον μαχόμενοι ἐπαύσαντο πρὶν ἀπέκτειναν τὸν τῶν πολεμίων στρατηγόν.

Exercises

A

1   When the king died, his daughter became queen.
2   They decided not to set out until darkness came on.
3   Before dying the old man gave a lot of money to his friends.
4   We will not let the hostages go until you promise never again to invade our country.
5   All must pay attention whenever the teacher is speaking.
6   When the Thebans heard what had happened, they sent a messenger to ask the Spartans to come to their aid.
7   Stay in the house until your mother returns from the market-place.
8   All the time that I was reading in the house, my brothers were playing in the garden.
9   We considered the Thebans our friends until they invaded Attica.
10   When your father returns, boys, he will be very angry to learn that you have stolen your sister's money.

B

1   When Themistocles arrived in Sparta, he wasted a lot of time talking to the ephors.
2   Travelling is always difficult whenever there is deep snow.
3   Both my mother and my sister will always be in trouble as long as they owe money to their friends.
4   The young man who had wronged my neighbour fled before being put on trial.
5   I hope to travel to Greece again before I die.
6   'When I return home,' said the king, 'I shall reward my friends but punish my enemies.'
7   We won't be on friendly terms with the Spartans until they stop attacking our city.
8   Cimon's soldiers remained inactive in the camp until their allies at last arrived.

9   For as long as the islanders were honoured by the Athenians, they
     remained in the alliance.
10   Whenever he arrived in Athens, the citizens always greeted him as a
     friend.

C

For as long as Zenis was alive, he was satrap[1] of Aeolis. But when he had
died of an illness, and someone else was going to take over the satrapy, his
wife, called Mania, displeased at this, fitted out an expedition[2] and set out
for the court of[3] Pharnabazus. On arrival she spoke as follows: 'My husband,
Pharnabazus, was friendly to you for many years and always paid his taxes;
if therefore I serve you no worse than he, there will be no need at all to
appoint someone else as satrap; but if in any way I do not satisfy you, it will
be in your power to give my position to another.' Hearing this, Pharnabazus
realised that the woman should be satrap; and she, once she had become
mistress[4] of the land, both paid her taxes, just as she had promised, and, in
addition, whenever she came to visit Pharnabazus' court, always brought
many gifts, in order to gratify both the governor himself and his
concubines[5]. When, however, Mania was only forty years of age[6], her son-
in-law, Midias, wishing to rule himself, but realising that he would never be
satrap until Mania died, is said to have gone in and throttled[7] her.

[1] he was satrap of: use σατραπεύω with genitive. (A satrap was a
provincial governor in the Persian empire.)

[2] Use στόλον ἀναζεύγνυμι (aor. ἀνέζευξα) = I fit out an expedition.

[3] to the court of = παρά with accusative.

[4] mistress: use the appropriate part of the adjective κύριος -α -ον
(= having power over, with genitive).

[5] concubine = παλλακή -ῆς ἡ.

[6] was forty years of age = had forty years.

[7] I throttle = ἀποπνίγω (aor. ἀπέπνιξα).

Chapter 21: Impersonal verbs; Accusative absolute; Gerundives

Impersonal verbs

An impersonal verb is one whose subject in English is *it*, e.g. *it pleases, it concerns, it is raining*. Greek has a number of impersonal verbs; we have already made use of some of the most common of them.

• With the accusative and infinitive:

δεῖ	it is necessary
χρή	it is necessary (NB *impf.* ἐχρῆν or χρῆν)

These verbs are the most common way to express obligation in Greek.

> *It is necessary for the slave to untie the horse.*
> = *The slave must/ought to untie the horse.*
> δεῖ τὸν δοῦλον λῦσαι τὸν ἵππον.

> *The slave ought to have untied the horse.*
> = lit. *It was necessary for the slave to untie the horse.*
> ἐχρῆν τὸν δοῦλον λῦσαι τὸν ἵππον.

• With the dative and infinitive:

δοκεῖ	it seems good
πρέπει	it is fitting, appropriate
προσήκει	it concerns
συμφέρει	it is advantageous, of use
λυσιτελεῖ	it is profitable
ἔξεστι(ν)	it is possible, permitted
πάρεστι(ν)	it is possible, permitted

> *It is to our advantage to return to the city.*
> συμφέρει ἡμῖν ἐπανελθεῖν πρὸς τὴν πόλιν.

It is not possible to do this.
οὐκ ἔξεστι τοῦτο ποιεῖν.

It seemed good to the general to retreat.
= The general decided to retreat.
ἔδοξε τῷ στρατηγῷ ἀναχωρῆσαι.

• With a dative of the person and a genitive of the thing:

μέτεστί μοι τούτου   I have a share in this
μέλει μοι τουτου   I care for this
μεταμέλει μοι τούτου   I'm sorry for this

• As in English, Greek uses impersonal verbs to describe weather conditions.
Note particularly the following:

ὕει   it is raining
νίφει   it is snowing
χειμάζει   it is stormy
βροντᾷ   there's thunder
ἀστράπτει   there's lightning

• There are many other impersonal expressions, consisting, usually, of a
neuter adjective and ἐστί. Note particularly the following:

δύνατόν ἐστι   it is possible
ἀδύνατόν ἐστι   it is impossible
δῆλόν ἐστι   it is clear
ἀδηλόν ἐστι   it is unclear
ἡμέτερόν ἐστι   it is our duty, our part
ἡμῶν ἐστι   it is our duty, our part

It is the duty of wise men to honour the gods.
τῶν σοφῶν ἐστι τιμᾶν τοὺς θεούς.

Accusative absolute

Impersonal verbs and expressions use an accusative absolute, in the neuter singular, rather than a genitive absolute. Particularly common examples are:

δέον   it being necessary
ἐξόν   it being possible
παρόν   it being possible
προσῆκον   it concerning
δόξαν   it having been resolved

It being necessary to capture the city, they drew up their forces at once.
δέον λαβεῖν τὴν πόλιν, εὐθὺς ἔταξαν τοὺς στρατιώτας.

After this, although it was possible to stay (i.e. although they could have stayed) on the island, they sailed away.
μετὰ ταῦτα, καίπερ παρὸν μένειν ἐν τῇ νήσῳ, ἀπέπλευσαν.

It being impossible to retreat, they continued fighting.
ἀδύνατον ὂν ἀναχωρῆσαι, μαχόμενοι διετέλουν.

Gerundives

As well as δεῖ and χρή, the verbal adjective or gerundive may be used to express obligation. The gerundive is usually formed by adding the endings -τέος -τέα -τέον to the stem of the aorist passive, with φ changing to π, and χ to κ, e.g:

παύω → ἐ-παύσ-θην → παυστέος
λαμβάνω → ἐ-λήφ-θην → ληπτέος
πράττω → ἐ-πράχ-θην → πρακτέος.

Note the following two irregular gerundives:

φέρω → οἰστέος   εἶμι → ἰτέος

There are two constructions.

i)   In the **personal construction**, which may be used only with transitive verbs (i.e. those which have a direct object in the accusative), the gerundive is used with εἰμί and is <u>passive</u> in sense. The agent, if expressed, goes in the dative.

> *We must help this city.* = *This city is to be helped by us.*
> αὕτη ἡ πόλις ἡμῖν ἐστιν ὠφελητέα.

> *The soldiers had to capture the fugitives.*
> οἱ φυγάδες ληπτέοι ἦσαν τοῖς στρατιώταις.

ii)   In the **impersonal construction**, the more common of the two, the gerundive is in the nominative neuter (either singular or plural) along with ἐστί or ἦν. Used like this the gerundive is practically <u>active</u> in sense and can take an object in whatever case the verb in question requires. Verbs which take the genitive or dative must use the impersonal construction. The agent is again regularly in the dative, though the accusative is possible as well.

> *We must come to the aid of our allies.*
> βοηθητέον ἐστὶν ἡμῖν τοῖς συμμάχοις.

> *The slaves had to untie the oxen.*
> λυτέα ἦν τοῖς δούλοις τοὺς βοῦς.

With both constructions the part of εἰμί is regularly omitted.

There is also a second verbal adjective, ending in -τός. It generally expresses capability, e.g. ἀκουστός = *capable of being heard, audible*; πρακτός = *capable of being done, practical*.

Exercises

A

1. It is never fitting for fathers to teach their own children.
2. Since it was necessary (= it being necessary) to take the bridge before nightfall, the army advanced as quickly as it could.
3. Students are not permitted to come into the teachers' room.
4. All should honour those who have died for Greece.
5. The Persians thought that it was to their advantage to subdue both Attica and Euboea.
6. The Athenians resolved to put Socrates to death on the grounds of having corrupted the young.
7. Since it was no longer possible (=it being no longer possible) to resist, they knew that the city had to be surrendered to the enemy.
8. It was unclear to us whether our friends wanted to return to Athens or not.
9. As it is to our advantage to have some respite from our labours, for my part I think that we should remain here for a long time.
10. The slaves were sorry for what they had done.

B

1. It isn't appropriate to stay out in the open whenever it is snowing.
2. As I am sorry for my stupidity, I hope that I will become your friend again, just as before.
3. It is the part of a sensible man to forgive those who do wrong.
4. The doctor must be sent for at once; for my wife is very ill.
5. On hearing the words of the jurors, he tried to depart immediately, as if it were not necessary for him to defend himself.
6. Our allies must by no means be handed over to the Spartans.
7. The Athenians have no part in this matter.
8. Although they might have escaped, all the Persians were killed in the battle.

9   The Spartans think that it is in their interest not to send out Pausanias
     as admiral.
10   The politician said that foreigners should never be despised.

C   (revision)

1   It was announced that the Athenians had been defeated in the sea-
     battle.
2   If the enemy besiege the city, many of the citizens will die before our
     allies arrive.
3   One ought never to go out into the garden whenever it is raining.
4   Things are now so bad that they cannot get any worse.
5   If my friend had not arrived at the critical moment, I should have
     perished in the river.
6   On his arrival the herald learned that the king's enemies had already
     been put to death.
7   Demosthenes and his men were hurrying along the road in order to get
     to Athens before nightfall.
8   If the teacher had understood the poem himself, he would have
     explained it better to his pupils.
9   When they saw what had happened, some of the citizens remained in
     the market-place, others ran away.
10   Who does not know that it is in everyone's interest to learn the Greek
     language?

D

After attacking Byzantium while it was still under Persian control[1],
Pausanias both captured the city and took prisoner some of the king's
relatives. And though it would have been possible[2] for him either to
imprison them or to put them to death, he sent them back to the king without
telling[3] the other Greeks, writing also a letter as follows: 'Pausanias the
leader of Sparta sends back these men, wishing to do you a favour, and at the
same time seeking your daughter's hand in marriage[4]. I am perfectly sure

that it is in your interest to accept my proposals; for in this way I intend to bring both Sparta and the rest of Greece under your dominion.'

On receipt of this letter Xerxes was overjoyed, and thinking that all this should happen[5] as quickly as possible, he wrote back to Pausanias, urging him to waste no time and promising to provide both money and soldiers. And Pausanias, who was already held in high esteem[6] by the Greeks on account of his victory at Plataea[7], then became so high and mighty[8] that he both dressed in Persian clothes and marched about the city with an Egyptian bodyguard. And he vented[9] such anger on everyone alike that it was no longer possible for anyone to approach him without fear.

[1] while it was still under Persian control: use a genitive absolute = the Persians still holding (it).

[2] though it would have been possible: use an accusative absolute from πάρεστι.

[3] without telling = κρύφα with genitive.

[4] seeking your daughter's hand in marriage = seeking to marry your daughter.

[5] that all this should happen: use gerundive = that all these things should be done.

[6] to be held in high esteem = ἐν μεγάλῳ ἀξιώματι εἶναι.

[7] at Plataea = Πλαταιᾶσι(ν).

[8] high and mighty: use σεμνός -ή -όν.

[9] he vented...upon: use χρῆσθαι (with dative) εἰς (with accusative).

Appendix 1: Passages from North and Hillard

For well over a hundred years the standard textbook in the English-speaking world for those wishing to learn to write Greek has been North and Hillard's Greek Prose Composition, *first published in 1898. So that the best of their passages, many of them by now 'old favourites' with teachers, aren't forgotten, we print here a selection of them, both as a homage to our predecessors, and as a useful supplement to our own passages. To fit with the order of constructions in our book, North and Hillard's original sequence has been slightly altered.*

Exercise 40 (after *WG*, Chapter 10)

When the Persians reached Marathon, ten thousand Athenians were drawn up on the mountains, under the command of Miltiades[1]. When they were about to attack the Persians, an army of one thousand infantry arrived from Plataea, the other states sending no soldiers. These Plataeans came, being grateful to the Athenians, who had helped them of old. Therefore eleven thousand Greeks were ready to attack the great host of the Persians. It was possible for them to remain in the mountains, but Miltiades ordered them to fall upon the Persians at once, whilst they were disembarking from their ships, and not fearing an attack.

[1] Miltiades being general (gen. abs.).

Exercise 46 (after *WG*, Chapter 11)

News came to Athens[1] that the Persians had already crossed the mountains, and were advancing into Attica. Many of the chief men speaking in the senate said that they would be unable to defend the city, and they thought it better to take refuge in the Acropolis; but on the advice of Themistocles[2] the majority determined to embark on the fleet[3], for they hoped that there they would be safe, thinking that the ships were the wooden walls spoken of[4] by the god.

[1] It was reported to (εἰς) Athens.   [3] ships

[2] Themistocles advising (gen. abs.).   [4] εἰρημένα

Exercise 56 (after *WG*, Chapter 12)

The messengers having returned, the general asked them what kind of country they had seen. They replied that it was a good land where fruit is gathered from the trees twice in the year, and that there were many rivers in it. When asked if the people had received them kindly, they answered that they had passed through the country and had suffered no harm; but that the people spoke a strange language, and they were not able to understand what they were saying. When the general asked how large the army of this people was, the messengers said they had not seen a soldier in all their journey.

Exercise 76 (after *WG*, Chapter 13)

Alcmaeon, being commanded by the god to leave his native land, set out, not knowing whither he was going. At Delphi, however, the Pythia told him not to despair because he was sent to another country, but to go to Achelous and ask the river-god to help him. When Alcmaeon came to the river, Achelous asked what he wanted. Alcmaeon replied that he was not allowed by the gods, who wished to punish him, to remain in his own land, and that the foreign lands to which he went were not willing to receive him. Then Achelous commanded the river to bring down sand and earth from the mountains, and in this way made a new land in which he allowed Alcmaeon to live.

Exercise 78 (after *WG*, Chapter 13)

After this the Trojans came at sunset to the land of the Cyclopes. Here they met a Greek who had been left behind by Ulysses. Aeneas bade him tell who he was and what had befallen him. The man replied that he was one of the sailors who were returning home from Troy after the war, and that when his companions escaped he alone had been left in the cave of the Cyclops. He begged Aeneas not to leave him in the island, where he ran the risk of being killed or dying of hunger. While he was speaking, the Trojans saw the shepherd Polyphemus coming down to the shore, and taking the suppliant, they speedily embarked on their ship and sailed away.

Exercise 96 (after *WG*, Chapter 15)

After the death of Cadmus many more people came to live in the Cadmea. Here they built many houses, so that at length they made a large city which they called Thebes. The Cadmea became the citadel of Thebes, and the king bade the citizens fortify it with very strong walls, in order that when an enemy attacked the city the inhabitants might take refuge in the citadel. There was once a king of Thebes called Amphion, who sang so beautifully that all things were compelled to obey him, and even the stones used to follow him. Knowing this he began to sing in the middle of the city, and so many stones came together to hear him sing that in a short time a stone wall was built round the city.

Exercise 109 (after *WG*, Chapter 16)

When the army had been drawn up for battle, the general thus addressed his soldiers: 'If we were now about to fight in a foreign country to increase our own possessions, the gods would perhaps be on the side of the enemy. But if the gods help men who are defending their native land, they ought now at least to be helping us. In the days of our fathers the Greeks would never have conquered the Persians if the gods had not been on their side; and our present enemies have shown themselves even more impious than the Persians. If, then, we fight bravely, believing that the gods will help us, we shall conquer.'

Exercise 128 (after *WG*, Chapter 17)

The army being thus dispirited, Xenophon alone appeared to be of good courage, though he himself did not hope to see Greece again. For now that for a little time the barbarians had ceased from their attacks, the mountains which they saw in front terrified them. Xenophon therefore went about among the soldiers exhorting them. To the captains he said: 'The army chose you to be captains after the death of Clearchus, supposing that you were the bravest and most ready to suffer hardship of us all. If you now show yourselves disheartened, how shall I encourage the rest?' To the soldiers he spoke thus: 'If a man were to ask me, comrades, why you are so disheartened, I could not answer him; nor would Cyrus have led you from Sardis to Babylon if he had known you were such men. You have passed through the greater dangers, the less remain. Yet, as if you were not the same men who defeated the Persians, you now shudder at mountains and wild beasts.'

Exercise 95 (after *WG*, Chapter 18)

Thus the Athenian fleet won a victory, and the Lacedaemonians were so disheartened that they no longer tried to besiege Mytilene. But in the battle a great number of the Athenians had perished, and when the Lacedaemonians sailed away many were still seen clinging to the wrecks. The generals therefore, determining themselves to follow the enemy, left certain ships behind and gave orders that these men should be saved. But a storm immediately arising, the officers of these ships, fearing that their own vessels might suffer harm, sailed away. When the news of this came to Athens the people ordered that the generals should be put on trial, and they were too enraged to listen to their defence. To escape the penalty two of the generals never returned, but those who had returned were put to death.

Exercise 114 (after *WG*, Chapter 18)

When many years had passed, there came a messenger to Thebes to tell Oedipus that King Polybus was dead, and to beg him to return to Corinth and be king of the city. But Oedipus would not return on account of the oracle; for though the king was dead, the queen was still alive, and he feared that some madness might compel him to desire to marry her. He told this to the messenger who happened to be the herdsman who had found Oedipus in the forest when he was a child. Then the old man, as if he were doing the king a service, informed him that he was not the son of Polybus, but had been found on Mount Cithaeron with his feet tied[1] with a string.

[1] tied as to his feet.

Exercise 148 (after *WG*, Chapter 19)

There was nothing now to save[1] the whole force from destruction. The fact
that Nicias had prevented the army from setting out, while there was still
hope of escape, had given fresh confidence to the enemy and filled the
Greek soldiers with rage and despair[2]. At this crisis[3] Nicias did his best to
cheer and encourage the men, though he was well aware that no one was to
blame but himself. He implored them not to despair, and asserted that for his
own part he did not believe that the Syracusans could prevent their reaching
the coast even if they endured many hardships on the march. But in reality
he hardly hoped to persuade anyone by such words; and though all were
ready to do whatever he ordered, there probably was not a man who did not
know that their case was hopeless.

[1] Use ἐμποδών.

[2] Say: knowing that Nicias … , the enemy were the more confident and the
Greeks more enraged, etc.

[3] The danger being so great.

Exercise 143 (after *WG,* Chapter 20)

Immediately after they had started they were delayed by adverse winds, and
put into the bay of Pylos until the wind should cease. Before starting,
Demosthenes had proposed to the Athenians to fortify some place in
Laconian territory; and now that the opportunity had come, he begged the
other generals, when they themselves sailed on to Sicily, to leave him in
command of even a few hoplites at Pylos. While the whole fleet was still
present, the sailors and marines built a small fort; when the rest departed,
Demosthenes, with a few hoplites, was left to defend it. As soon as the news
reached Sparta, a force was sent to take Pylos; but the fort was already too
strong to be taken easily.

Exercise 156 (after *WG*, Chapter 21)

Nicias had drawn up the Athenians on the right wing and the Sicilian allies on the left, where, on account of the hill, they were not likely to share in the contest; for he greatly feared that if the Athenians were worsted the Sicilians would desert to the enemy. But before the battle began he addressed the Athenians as follows: 'Men of Athens, you perceive for yourselves in what danger we lie, and I know that I myself am responsible for it. But let all of you recall to mind the great deeds of our ancestors who put to flight the Persians at Marathon. Would that Miltiades were here to lead us today! But so far as I am able I shall do what becomes a general, and I believe the gods will be on our side.'

Exercise 168 (after *WG*, Chapter 21)

Meanwhile the king, having taken up his position, as has been said, in the centre, and seeing no one coming against him, advanced as if to attack the Greeks on their flank. Cyrus, seeing this, charged at full speed with his six hundred, and broke the line in front of the king. The troopers were scattered in the ardour of pursuit[1], and Cyrus was left alone with a handful of men. Even so, all would have been well, if he had not suddenly caught sight of his brother. But on perceiving him in the throng, he cried out, 'There is the man!' and advanced furiously against him. The two brothers engaged at once in a hand-to-hand struggle. But Cyrus and his followers were too few to be victorious. Before long they were hurled to the ground, and Cyrus himself with eight others was slain.

[1] pursuing with great eagerness.

Appendix 2: Uses of the subjunctive and optative

Subjunctive	Optative

Subjunctive

Main Clauses

Deliberative questions, direct
(Chapter 12)
Exhortations (Chapter 13)
Prohibitions (Chapter 13)

Subordinate Clauses

Purpose clauses in either primary
or historic sequence (Chapter 14)
Protasis (with ἐάν) of open
future conditions (Chapter 16)

Fearing clauses in either primary
or historic sequence (Chapter 18)
Sometimes after verbs of precaution
in either primary or historic
sequence (Chapter 18)
With ἄν in indefinite and temporal
clauses in primary sequence
(Chapters 19 & 20)

Deliberative questions, indirect
(Chapter 12)

Optative

Main Clauses

Wishes for the future (Chapter 13)

With ἄν in potential statements
(Chapter 16)

Subordinate Clauses

Purpose clauses in historic sequence
(Chapter 14)
Protasis (with εἰ) and apodosis
(with ἄν) of unreal future conditions
(Chapter 16)
Fearing clauses in historic sequence
(Chapter 18)
Sometimes after verbs of precaution
in historic sequence (Chapter 18)

Without ἄν in indefinite and
temporal clauses in historic
sequence (Chapters 19 & 20)
Indirect statements in historic
sequence (Chapter 11)
Indirect questions in historic sequence
(Chapter 12)
Subordinate clauses in indirect speech
(Chapter 13)

Appendix 3: Negatives and their main uses

The simple negatives in Greek are οὐ and μή. As a general rule, οὐ is the negative of facts and statements, and μή the negative of ideas and concepts.

οὐ is used in/with:

• all direct statements;
• all indirect statements, whether using the indicative, optative, infinitive or participle, except those using the infinitive after verbs of *hoping, promising* etc. and verbs of *confident assertion* (Chapter 11);
• direct questions expecting the answer *yes*, and in normal indirect questions (Chapter 12);
• result clauses with the indicative (Chapter 15);
• the normal apodosis of conditional sentences (Chapter 16);
• definite relative and temporal clauses (Chapters 9 and 20);
• the participle when it makes a statement (Chapters 6 and 17).

μή is used in/with:

• all commands, exhortations and wishes (Chapter 13);
• direct questions expecting the answer *no*, and in all deliberative questions (Chapter 12);
• indirect questions after εἰ, and in the second part of indirect double questions (Chapter 12);
• result clauses with the infinitive (Chapter 15);
• purpose clauses with the subjunctive, optative or future indicative (Chapter 14);
• the protasis of all conditional sentences (Chapter 16);
• indefinite relative and temporal clauses (Chapters 19 and 20);
• generic relative clauses (see below);
• the infinitive except in indirect statements (but see above);
• the participle with conditional force (Chapter 17) or with generic force (see below).

The following are the most common compound negatives:

οὐδείς οὐδεμία οὐδέν	μηδείς μηδεμία μηδέν	no one
οὐ ... ποτέ	μὴ ... ποτέ	never
οὔποτε	μήποτε	never
οὐδέποτε	μηδέποτε	never
οὐκέτι	μηκέτι	no longer
οὔπω	μήπω	not yet
οὐδέ	μηδέ	and not, not even
οὔτε...οὔτε	μήτε...μήτε	neither ... nor
οὐδαμῶς	μηδαμῶς	in no way

Generic μή

μή may be used both with the indicative and with participles to describe a class or type, rather than particular people or things.

He teaches the boys the type of things which they don't know.
διδάσκει τοὺς παῖδας ἃ μὴ ἴσασιν.

The type of people who know nothing always please the authorities.
οἱ μηδὲν εἰδότες ἀεὶ ἀρέσκουσι τοῖς ἐν τέλει.

These sentences contrast with:

He is teaching the boys these things which they don't know.
διδάσκει τοὺς παῖδας ταῦτα ἃ οὐκ ἴσασιν.

These people who know nothing are very troublesome.
οὗτοι οἱ οὐδὲν εἰδότες μάλιστά εἰσιν ὀχληροί.

Repeated negatives

A compound negative following another negative (simple or compound) confirms it rather than cancelling it.

> *Never do such things.*
> μὴ τοιαῦτα πράττε μηδέποτε.

If however a simple negative follows a compound, the two cancel each other out.

> *Everybody does this.*
> οὐδεὶς ταῦτα οὐ πράττει.

Double negatives

i) The uses of the double negative μὴ οὐ after verbs of fearing and precaution and of preventing, hindering and denying are explained in Chapter 18.

ii) οὐ μή with the aorist subjunctive (less commonly the present) or with the future indicative expresses an emphatic negative statement.

> *I shall certainly not cease from praising the gods.*
> οὐ μὴ παύσωμαι (παύσομαι) ἐπαινῶν τοὺς θεούς.

Appendix 4: Prepositions

	+ *accusative*	+ *genitive*	+ *dative*
ἅμα			at the same time as *at daybreak* ἅμ' ἡμέρᾳ
ἀμφί	around *Xenophon and his men* οἱ ἀμφὶ τὸν Ξενοφῶντα		
ἀνά	up, throughout *up stream* ἀνὰ ποταμόν *throughout the day* ἀνὰ τὴν ἡμέραν		
ἄνευ		without *without water* ἄνευ ὕδατος	
ἀντί		instead of *water instead of wine* ὕδωρ ἀντὶ οἴνου	
ἀπό		from *from the city* ἀπὸ τῆς πόλεως	

Prepositions

	+ *accusative*	+ *genitive*	+ *dative*
διά	on account of	through	

on account of fear
διὰ φόβον

through the fields
διὰ τῶν ἀγρῶν

after a short time
δι' ὀλίγου

every five years
διὰ πέντε ἐτῶν

εἰς   into

into the garden
εἰς τὸν κῆπον

up to a hundred
εἰς ἑκατόν

at the right time
εἰς καιρόν

ἐκ (ἐξ before vowel)   out of, from

out of the house
ἐκ τῆς οἰκίας

after this
ἐκ τούτου

equally
ἐξ ἴσου

	+ *accusative*	+ *genitive*	+ *dative*
ἐν			in, at, among
			in the village ἐν τῇ κώμῃ
			among the Spartans ἐν τοῖς Λακεδαιμονίοις
			meanwhile ἐν τούτῳ

ἕνεκα		on account of (*follows noun*)	
		on account of money χρημάτων ἕνεκα	

ἐπί	towards, against	on, in the time of	on, upon
	against the wall ἐπὶ τὸ τεῖχος	*on horseback* ἐφ' ἵππου	*on these terms* ἐπὶ τούτοις
		in the time of Homer ἐπὶ τοῦ Ὁμήρου	

κατά	down, according to, throughout, by	down from	
	downstream κατὰ ποταμόν	*down from the mountain* κατὰ τοῦ ὄρους	
	according to custom κατὰ τὸν νόμον		
	by land κατὰ γήν		

Prepositions

	+ *accusative*	+ *genitive*	+ *dative*
μετά	after	with	
	after this μετὰ ταῦτα	*with the allies* μετὰ τῶν συμμάχων	

παρά	along, beside, into the presence of, contrary to	from (*a person*)	beside, with (*a person*)
	before Cyrus παρὰ τὸν Κῦρον	*from Cyrus* παρὰ τοῦ Κύρου	*with Cyrus* παρὰ τῷ Κύρῳ
	along the road παρὰ τὴν ὁδόν		
	contrary to the laws παρὰ τοὺς νόμους		

περί	around, about	concerning	
	around the walls περὶ τὰ τείχη	*concerning the gods* περὶ τῶν θεῶν	
	around 1000 περὶ χιλίους	*to regard as important* περὶ πολλοῦ ποιεῖσθαι	
	Xenophon and his men οἱ περὶ τὸν Ξενοφῶντα		

πλήν		except	
		except one πλὴν ἑνός	

πρό		before, in front of	
		before the war πρὸ τοῦ πολέμου	

	+ *accusative*	+ *genitive*	+ *dative*
πρός	to, towards	from, at the hands of, in the name of	near, in addition to
	towards the shore πρὸς τὴν ἀκτήν	*at whose hands?* πρὸς τίνος;	*in addition to these things* πρὸς τούτοις
		in the name of the gods πρὸς τῶν θέων	
σύν			with, with the help of
			with the help of the gods σὺν τοῖς θεοῖς
ὑπέρ	beyond	above, on behalf of	
	beyond hope ὑπὲρ ἐλπίδα	*on behalf of the city* ὑπὲρ τῆς πόλεως	
ὑπό	under, to under, about the time of	by (*a person*)	under, subject to
	led under the yoke ὑπὸ ζύγον ἀχθείς	*by the Persians* ὑπὸ τῶν Περσῶν	*subject to the Athenians* ὑπὸ τοῖς Ἀθηναίοις
	just before nightfall ὑπὸ νύκτα		
ὡς	to (a person)		
	to the magistrate ὡς τὸν ἄρχοντα		

Appendix 5: Accents

Accents are universally printed in Greek texts, but were not used in classical Athens: they seem to have been introduced in Alexandria about 200 BC, to help non-native speakers of Greek with pronunciation, and to clarify ambiguities (distinguishing otherwise identical words). The rules for their use are simple in outline but complex in detail. It is not essential for beginners in writing Greek to include them (the interrogative τίς is a conventional exception) but if you wish to do so this appendix, adapted from the equivalent one in North and Hillard (see Appendix 1 of this book), should help. For more detail, readers are referred to Philomen Probert *A New Short Guide to the Accentuation of Ancient Greek* (BCP 2003).

• There are three accents. They strictly indicate musical pitch rather than stress, though this is difficult for English speakers to reproduce.

acute	´	high
grave	`	low
circumflex	^	high falling to low

• The acute on the last syllable of a word is changed to grave when another word follows (this is the only situation in which the grave is used), unless that word is an enclitic (see below), in which case the acute remains.

• Words with accents in particular places have technical names.

accent	*syllable*	*word is called*
acute	last	oxytone
acute	second-last	paroxytone
acute	third-last	proparoxytone
grave	last	barytone
circumflex	last	perispomenon
circumflex	second-last	properispomenon

• If a diphthong has an accent, it stands on the second of the two vowels.

General rules

1   Position of acute and circumflex

The acute can stand on long or short syllables, the circumflex only on syllables containing a vowel long by nature or a diphthong. The acute can stand on any of the last three syllables, the circumflex only on the last or second-last. But if the last syllable is long, the acute cannot stand on the third-last, or the circumflex on the second-last. Hence e.g. ἄνθρωπος but ἀνθρώπου.

No accent can stand further back than the third-last syllable of a long word.

In words of which the last syllable is short and the second-last long by nature, if the accent is on the second-last it must be circumflex. Hence e.g. δῶρον, τεῖχος.

2   Contracted syllables

Contracted syllables have the circumflex when the <u>first</u> of the two syllables in uncontracted form was accented. Hence e.g. φιλέω becomes φιλῶ. They have the acute when the <u>second</u> syllable was accented. Hence e.g. φιλεέτω becomes φιλείτω. They are unaccented if neither of the two syllables was accented. Hence e.g. φίλεε becomes φίλει.

3   Enclitics

Certain words called *enclitics* (literally *leaning on* another) lose their accent by being pronounced in close connection with the previous word. Enclitics are:

i	All forms of the indefinite τις.
ii	The indefinite adverbs πως, που, ποτε etc.

iii   Certain cases of personal pronouns: με, μου, μοι, σε, σου, σοι.

iv   The present indicative of εἰμί *I am** and φημί *I say* (except 2 sing.).

v   The particles τε, γε, τοι, νυν, περ.

* The whole present of εἰμί is accented when it denotes *existence*; 3 sing. is accented on the first syllable (ἔστι) when it denotes existence; when it means *it is possible* (= ἔξεστι); when it starts a sentence; and when it comes after εἰ, καί, οὐκ, ὡς.

Rules for enclitics:

i   If the preceding word is oxytone it retains the acute accent; if it is perispomenon, the enclitic loses its accent with no other change. Hence e.g. ἀγαθός τις, ὁδῶν τινων.

ii   If the preceding word is paroxytone, a monosyllabic enclitic loses its accent with no other change, but an enclitic of two syllables keeps its accent. Hence e.g. λόγος τις, λόγοι τινές.

iii   If the preceding word is proparoxytone or properispomenon, the accent of the enclitic is thrown back as an acute on the last syllable. Hence e.g. τοῦτό μοι ἔδωκέ τις.

iv   When several enclitics follow one another, each throws its accent back so that only the last is unaccented. Hence e.g. εἴ ποτέ πού τι εἶδον.

4   Atonics

A few words are *atonic* (have no accent), unless they are followed by an enclitic or come last in a sentence, notably masculine and feminine nominative parts of the article ὁ, ἡ, οἱ, αἱ; the negative οὐ; εἰ (= *if*); εἰς, ἐκ, ἐν, and ὡς (= *how, to,* or *when / as / that*).

5   Anastrophe

Anastrophe (literally *throwing back* the accent within a word) occurs:

i   When a two-syllable preposition (other than ἀμφί, ἀντί, ἀνά, διά) comes after its noun. Hence e.g. τούτων πέρι (instead of usual περί).

ii   When an oxytone word is elided, unless it is indeclinable. Hence e.g. δείν' ἔπαθε (for δεινὰ ἔπαθε), but ἐπ' αὐτοῦ.

6   Accents on verbs

• Generally the accent stands as far back as possible. Hence e.g. ἔλυσε, ἐλύθην, λῦσαι.

• Final syllables -αι and -οι are treated as short except in the optative. Hence e.g. λῦσαι (infinitive) but λύσαι (optative).

• Contracted forms are accented according to Rule 2 above.

The following are treated as contracted forms: (1) all aorist passive subjunctives, hence e.g. λυθῶ; present and second aorist subjunctive and optative forms of -μι verbs (except ones ending -νυμι), hence e.g. τιθῶ, τιθεῖμεν, θῶ, θεῖσθε.

Exceptions:
i   The second aorist is accented on the last syllable in the active infinitive and participle, and 2 sing. middle imperative, and on the second-last in the middle infinitive. Hence e.g. λαβεῖν, λαβών -οῦσα -όν, λαβοῦ, λαβέσθαι.

ii   The following second aorist imperatives are oxytone: εἰπέ, ἐλθέ, εὑρέ, ἰδέ, λαβέ.

iii   The following parts of verbs are paroxytone if the second-last syllable is short, properispomenon if it is long:
- first aorist active infinitive, hence e.g. τιμῆσαι, πλέξαι;
- all infinitives in -ναι, hence e.g. τιθέναι, λελυκέναι, στῆναι;
- all perfect passive infinitives and participles, hence e.g. τετιμῆσθαι, λελυμένος.

iv   Active participles of -μι verbs and all others ending -εις and -ως are oxytone, hence e.g. τιθείς, λυθείς, λελυκώς.

v   In compound verbs the accent may not go back:
- beyond the augment, hence e.g. παρέσχον, κατῆγον;
- beyond the last syllable of the prefix, hence e.g. ἀπόδος, ἐπίσχες (but note exceptions ἄπειμι, πάρεστι, ἄπιθι etc);
- beyond the verbal part of infinitives and participles of -μι verbs, hence e.g. ἀποδούς, ἀποδόσθαι; likewise not beyond the verbal part of 2 sing. middle imperative of -μι verbs with prefix of one syllable, hence e.g. προθοῦ but μετάδου.

7   Nouns and adjectives

• Nominative plurals -αι and -οι are treated as short.

• The accent on the oblique cases generally remains on the same syllable as in the nominative, so far as Rule 1 allows. Hence e.g. ἄνθρωπος, ἄνθρωπον, ἀνθρώπου.

• All genitives and datives of oxytone words of the first and second declensions are perispomena. Hence e.g. ὁδός, ὁδοῦ, ὁδοί, ὁδῶν (but in Attic second declension the acute is retained, e.g. λεώς, λεώ).

• In the first declension the genitive plural is perispomenon.

• In the third declension the genitive and dative of monosyllabic words are normally accented on the last syllable, hence e.g. χείρ, χειρός, χεῖρες, χειρῶν (exceptions include participles, e.g. θείς, θέντος; τίς, τίνος; πᾶς, πάντων, πᾶσι; παῖς, παιδός, παίδων).

• In third declension words like πόλις and πῆχυς the endings -εως, -εων are treated as one syllable, hence e.g. πόλεως, πήχεων.

• No complete rules can be given for accenting the nominative singular, but the following are generally true.

i   Oxytone are:
- nouns ending -ευς (e.g. βασιλεύς), -ω (e.g. πειθώ), -ας with gen. -αδος (e.g. φυγάς), -ις if -ιδ- stem used for acc. (e.g. ἐλπίς);
- most adjectives ending -ρος (e.g. αἰσχρός), -νος (e.g. ἱκανός), -ης (e.g. ἀληθής), -υς (e.g. ἡδύς), -ικος (e.g. πρακτικός), verbal adjectives ending -τος (e.g. λυτός), adjectives meaning *good* or *bad* (e.g. ἀγαθός, κακός).

ii   Paroxytone are:
- most nouns ending -ια (e.g. δειλία);
- nouns formed from verbs and ending -τωρ (e.g. ῥήτωρ);
- patronymics (e.g. Ἀσκληπιάδης);
- verbal adjectives ending - τεος (e.g. λυτέος).

iii Proparoxytone are:
- nouns ending -εια except those formed from verbs ending -ευω (hence e.g. ἀλήθεια but δουλεία).

iv   Recessive (i.e. the accent goes back as far as possible) are:
- nouns formed from verbs and ending -μα (e.g. πρᾶγμα);
- neuter words ending -ος (e.g. μέγεθος);
- nouns ending -ις with acc. -ιν (e.g. δύναμις);
- comparatives and superlatives (e.g. καλλίων, ἄριστος);
- adjectives ending -ιμος (e.g. φρόνιμος).

Appendix 6: Principal parts of 100 important irregular verbs

present	meaning	future	aorist (* imperfect)
ἀγγέλλω	announce	ἀγγελῶ	ἤγγειλα
ἄγω	lead	ἄξω	ἤγαγον
αἱρέω αἱρέομαι	take choose	αἱρήσω αἱρήσομαι	εἷλον εἱλόμην
αἴρω	raise	ἀρῶ	ἦρα
αἰσθάνομαι	perceive	αἰσθήσομαι	ᾐσθόμην
αἰσχύνω	disgrace	αἰσχυνῶ	ᾔσχυνα
ἀκούω	hear	ἀκούσομαι	ἤκουσα
ἁμαρτάνω	miss the mark	ἁμαρτήσομαι	ἥμαρτον
ἀποθνῄσκω	die	ἀποθανοῦμαι	ἀπέθανον
ἀποκρίνομαι	answer	ἀποκρινοῦμαι	ἀπεκρινάμην
ἀποκτείνω	kill	ἀποκτενῶ	ἀπέκτεινα
ἀπόλλυμι	destroy, lose perish	ἀπολῶ ἀπολοῦμαι	ἀπώλεσα ἀπωλόμην
ἄρχω	rule begin	ἄρξω ἄρξομαι	ἦρξα ἠρξάμην
ἀφικνέομαι	arrive	ἀφίξομαι	ἀφικόμην
βαίνω	go	βήσομαι	ἔβην
βάλλω	throw	βαλῶ	ἔβαλον
βλάπτω	harm	βλάψω	ἔβλαψα

128

Principal parts of 100 important irregular verbs

perfect	perfect middle/passive	aorist passive (** active sense)	
ἤγγελκα	ἤγγελμαι	ἠγγέλθην	(announce)
ἦχα	ἦγμαι	ἤχθην	(lead)
ᾕρηκα	ᾕρημαι	ᾑρέθην	(take) (choose)
ἦρκα	ἦρμαι	ἤρθην	(raise)
-	ᾔσθημαι (*act. sense*)	-	(perceive)
-	-	ᾐσχύνθην	(disgrace)
ἀκήκοα	-	ἠκούσθην	(hear)
ἡμάρτηκα	ἡμάρτημαι	ἡμαρτήθην	(miss)
τέθνηκα	-	-	(die)
-	ἀποκέκριμαι	-	(answer)
ἀπέκτονα	-	-	(kill)
ἀπολώλεκα ἀπόλωλα	-	-	(destroy) (perish)
ἦρχα	ἦργμαι	ἤρχθην	(rule) (begin)
-	ἀφῖγμαι	-	(arrive)
βέβηκα	-	-	(go)
βέβληκα	βέβλημαι	ἐβλήθην	(throw)
βέβλαφα	βέβλαμμαι	ἐβλάβην	(harm)

129

Principal parts of 100 important irregular verbs

present	meaning	future	aorist (* imperfect)
βούλομαι	wish, want	βουλήσομαι	-
γαμέω	marry	γαμῶ	ἔγημα
γελάω	laugh	γελάσομαι	ἐγέλασα
γίγνομαι	become	γενήσομαι	ἐγενόμην
γιγνώσκω	get to know	γνώσομαι	ἔγνων
γράφω	write	γράψω	ἔγραψα
δεῖ	it is necessary	δεήσει	ἐδέησε(ν) ἔδει*
δείκνυμι	show	δείξω	ἔδειξα
δέχομαι	receive	δέξομαι	ἐδεξάμην
διαφθείρω	destroy	διαφθερῶ	διέφθειρα
διδάσκω	teach	διδάξω	ἐδίδαξα
δίδωμι	give	δώσω	ἔδωκα
διώκω	chase	διώξομαι	ἐδίωξα
δοκέω	seem, think	δόξω	ἔδοξα
δύναμαι	be able	δυνήσομαι	ἐδυνάμην*
ἐάω	allow	ἐάσω	εἴασα
ἐθέλω	be willing	ἐθελήσω	ἠθέλησα
εἰμί	be	ἔσομαι	ἦ*/ἦν*

Principal parts of 100 important irregular verbs

perfect	perfect middle/passive	aorist passive (** active sense)	
-	βεβούλημαι	ἐβουλήθην**	(wish, want)
γεγάμηκα	γεγάμημαι	-	(marry)
-	-	ἐγελάσθην	(laugh)
γέγονα	γεγένημαι	-	(become)
ἔγνωκα	ἔγνωσμαι	ἐγνώσθην	(get to know)
γέγραφα	γέγραμμαι	ἐγράφην	(write)
-	-	-	(it is necessary)
δέδειχα	δέδειγμαι	ἐδείχθην	(show)
-	δέδεγμαι	-εδέχθην	(receive)
διέφθαρκα	διέφθαρμαι	διεφθάρην	(destroy)
δεδίδαχα	δεδίδαγμαι	ἐδιδάχθην	(teach)
δέδωκα	δέδομαι	ἐδόθην	(give)
δεδίωχα	-	ἐδιώχθην	(chase)
-	δέδογμαι	-	(seem)
-	δεδύνημαι	ἐδυνήθην**	(be able)
εἴακα	εἴαμαι	εἰάθην	(allow)
ἠθέληκα	-	-	(be willing)
-	-	-	(be)

131

Principal parts of 100 important irregular verbs

present	meaning	future	aorist (* imperfect)
ἐλαύνω	drive	ἐλῶ (-άω)	ἤλασα
ἕλκω	drag	ἕλξω	εἵλκυσα
ἐλπίζω	hope	ἐλπιῶ	ἤλπισα
ἐπαινέω	praise	ἐπαινέσω	ἐπῄνεσα
ἐπίσταμαι	know how	ἐπιστήσομαι	ἠπιστάμην*
ἕπομαι	follow	ἕψομαι	ἑσπόμην
ἔρχομαι	go, come	εἶμι	ἦλθον
ἐρωτάω	ask	ἐρωτήσω ἐρήσομαι	ἠρώτησα ἠρόμην
ἐσθίω	eat	ἔδομαι	ἔφαγον
εὑρίσκω	find	εὑρήσω	ηὗρον εὗρον
ἔχω	have	ἕξω σχήσω	ἔσχον εἶχον*
ἥδομαι	enjoy	ἡσθήσομαι	-
θάπτω	bury	θάψω	ἔθαψα
θαυμάζω	be amazed	θαυμάσομαι	ἐθαύμασα
ἵημι	send, let go	ἥσω	ἧκα
ἵστημι	make stand stand	στήσω	ἔστησα ἔστην
καθεύδω	sleep	καθευδήσω	ἐκάθευδον* καθηῦδον*

perfect	perfect middle/passive	aorist passive (** active sense)	
ἐλήλακα	ἐλήλαμαι	ἠλάθην	(drive)
εἵλκυκα	εἵλκυσμαι	εἱλκύσθην	(drag)
ἤλπικα	-	ἠλπίσθην	(hope)
ἐπήνεκα	ἐπήνημαι	ἐπηνέθην	(praise)
-	-	ἠπιστήθην**	(know how)
-	-	-	(follow)
ἐλήλυθα	-	-	(go, come)
ἠρώτηκα	ἠρώτημαι	ἠρωτήθην	(ask)
ἐδήδοκα	ἐδήδεσμαι	ἠδέσθην	(eat)
ηὕρηκα εὕρηκα	ηὕρημαι εὕρημαι	ηὑρέθην εὑρέθην	(find)
ἔσχηκα	-έσχημαι	-	(have)
-	-	ἥσθην**	(enjoy)
-	τέθαμμαι	ἐτάφην	(bury)
τεθαύμακα	-	ἐθαυμάσθην	(be amazed)
εἶκα	εἶμαι	εἵθην	(send)
	-	ἐστάθην	(make stand)
ἔστηκα (I stand)			(stand)
-	-	-	(sleep)

present	meaning	future	aorist (* imperfect)
καθίζω	sit	καθιῶ	ἐκάθισα
καίω	burn	καύσω	ἔκαυσα
καλέω	call	καλῶ	ἐκάλεσα
κλέπτω	steal	κλέψω	ἔκλεψα
κόπτω	cut	κόψω	ἔκοψα
κρίνω	judge	κρινῶ	ἔκρινα
κτάομαι	obtain	κτήσομαι	ἐκτησάμην
λαμβάνω	take	λήψομαι	ἔλαβον
λανθάνω	escape notice	λήσω	ἔλαθον
λέγω	say	ἐρῶ λέξω	εἶπον ἔλεξα
λείπω	leave	λείψω	ἔλιπον
μανθάνω	learn	μαθήσομαι	ἔμαθον
μάχομαι	fight	μαχοῦμαι	ἐμαχεσάμην
μέλλω	be about to	μελλήσω	ἐμέλλησα
μένω	stay	μενῶ	ἔμεινα
νομίζω	think, consider	νομιῶ	ἐνόμισα
οἶδα	know	εἴσομαι	ᾔδη*
ὄμνυμι	swear	ὀμοῦμαι	ὤμοσα

Principal parts of 100 important irregular verbs

perfect	perfect middle/passive	aorist passive (** active sense)	
-	-	-	(sit)
κέκαυκα	κέκαυμαι	ἐκαύθην	(burn)
κέκληκα	κέκλημαι	ἐκλήθην	(call)
κέκλοφα	κέκλεμμαι	ἐκλάπην	(steal)
κέκοφα	κέκομμαι	ἐκόπην	(cut)
κέκρικα	κέκριμαι	ἐκρίθην	(judge)
-	κέκτημαι	ἐκτήθην	(obtain)
εἴληφα	εἴλημμαι	ἐλήφθην	(take)
λέληθα	λέλησμαι	-	(escape notice)
εἴρηκα	εἴρημαι λέλεγμαι	ἐρρήθην	(say)
λέλοιπα	λέλειμμαι	ἐλείφθην	(leave)
μεμάθηκα	-	-	(learn)
-	μεμάχημαι	-	(fight)
-	-	-	(be about to)
μεμένηκα	-	-	(stay)
νενόμικα	νενόμισμαι	ἐνομίσθην	(think)
-	-	-	(know)
ὀμώμοκα	-	ὠμό(σ)θην	(swear)

Principal parts of 100 important irregular verbs

present	meaning	future	aorist (* imperfect)
ὁράω	see	ὄψομαι	εἶδον ἑώρων*
πάσχω	suffer	πείσομαι	ἔπαθον
πείθω πειθομαι	persuade obey	πείσω πείσομαι	ἔπεισα ἐπιθόμην
πειράομαι	try	πειράσομαι	ἐπειρασάμην
πέμπω	send	πέμψω	ἔπεμψα
πίνω	drink	πίομαι	ἔπιον
πίπτω	fall	πεσοῦμαι	ἔπεσον
πλέω	sail	πλεύσομαι	ἔπλευσα
πράσσω	do, fare	πράξω	ἔπραξα
πυνθάνομαι	enquire, find out	πεύσομαι	ἐπυθόμην
σημαίνω	signal	σημανῶ	ἐσήμηνα
σκοπέω	look at	σκέψομαι	ἐσκεψάμην
στέλλω	send	στελῶ	ἔστειλα
σῴζω	save	σώσω	ἔσωσα
τάσσω	draw up	τάξω	ἔταξα
τέμνω	cut	τεμῶ	ἔτεμον
τίθημι	place, put	θήσω	ἔθηκα

Principal parts of 100 important irregular verbs

perfect	perfect middle/passive	aorist passive (** active sense)	
ἑώρακα	ἑώραμαι	ὤφθην	(see)
πέπονθα	-	-	(suffer)
πέπεικα	πέπεισμαι	ἐπείσθην	(persuade) (obey)
-	πεπείραμαι	ἐπειράθην**	(try)
πέπομφα	πέπεμμαι	ἐπέμφθην	(send)
πέπωκα	-	ἐπόθην	(drink)
πέπτωκα	-	-	(fall)
πέπλευκα	πέπλευσμαι	ἐπλεύσθην	(sail)
πέπραχα πέπραγα (I have fared)	πέπραγμαι	ἐπράχθην	(do, fare)
-	πέπυσμαι	-	(enquire)
-	σεσήμασμαι	ἐσημάνθην	(signal)
-	ἔσκεμμαι	-	(look at)
ἔσταλκα	ἔσταλμαι	ἐστάλην	(send)
σέσωκα	σέσωσμαι	ἐσώθην	(save)
τέταχα	τέταγμαι	ἐτάχθην	(draw up)
τέτμηκα	τέτμημαι	ἐτμήθην	(cut)
τέθηκα	-	ἐτέθην	(place)

Principal parts of 100 important irregular verbs

present	meaning	future	aorist (* imperfect)
τρέπω	turn	τρέψω	ἔτρεψα
τρέχω	run	δραμοῦμαι	ἔδραμον
τυγχάνω	chance	τεύξομαι	ἔτυχον
τύπτω	hit	τύψω	ἔτυψα
ὑπισχνέομαι	promise	ὑποσχήσομαι	ὑπεσχόμην
φαίνω	show	φανῶ	ἔφηνα
φαίνομαι	appear	φανοῦμαι	ἐφηνάμην
φέρω	carry	οἴσω	ἤνεγκα/ἤνεγκον
φέρομαι	win	οἴσομαι	ἠνεγκάμην
φεύγω	flee	φεύξομαι	ἔφυγον
φημί	say	φήσω	ἔφησα ἔφην*
φθάνω	do first	φθήσομαι	ἔφθασα ἔφθην
φοβέομαι	fear	φοβήσομαι	-
φυλάσσω	guard	φυλάξω	
χράομαι	use	χρήσομαι	ἐχρησάμην
χρή	it is necessary	-	χρῆν*/ἐχρῆν*

perfect	perfect middle/passive	aorist passive (** active sense)	
τέτροφα	τέτραμμαι		(turn)
δεδράμηκα	-	-	(run)
τετύχηκα	-	-	(chance)
-	-	ἐτύφθην	(hit)
-	ὑπέσχημαι	-	(promise)
πέφηνα	πέφασμαι	ἐφάνθην ἐφάνην**	(show) (appear)
ἐνήνοχα	ἐνήνεγμαι	ἠνέχθην	(carry) (win)
πέφευγα	-	-	(flee)
-	-	-	(say)
ἔφθακα	-	-	(do first)
-	πεφόβημαι	ἐφοβήθην**	(fear)
πεφύλαχα	πεφύλαγμαι	ἐφυλάχθην	(guard)
-	κέχρημαι	ἐχρήσθην	(use)
-	-	-	(it is necessary)

Vocabulary

The principal parts of verbs marked with an asterisk (*) can be found listed in Appendix 6. In the interests of space, the perfect tenses of other verbs have been given only when the exercises in the book require them.

abandon, I	ἀπολείπω (see λείπω*), καταλείπω
= I pass over, omit	παρίημι (see ἵημι*)
ability, to the best of one's	κατὰ δύναμιν
able, I am	δύναμαι*, οἷός τ' εἰμί (see εἰμί*)
about, around	κατά with accusative
about, concerning	περί with genitive
about to, I am	μέλλω* usually with future infinitive
above	ὑπέρ with genitive
abroad, I go	ἀποδημέω -ήσω -ησα
absolutely (nothing)	ἀτέχνως (οὐδέν)
accept, I	δέχομαι*
accidentally	τύχῃ, ἀκουσίως
accordingly	οὖν
account of, on	διά with accusative
accurate	ἀκριβής -ές
accuse, I	αἰτιάομαι -ασομαι ᾐτιασάμην (ᾐτιάθην in passive sense) with accusative of person and genitive of crime, κατηγορέω -ήσω -ησα with genitive of person and accusative of crime
Achelous	Ἀχελῷος -ου ὁ
Achilles	Ἀχιλλεύς -έως ὁ
acquire, I	κτάομαι*
Acropolis	ἀκρόπολις -εως ἡ
act, I	πράττω or πράσσω*
addition, in	πρὸς τούτοις
address, I	προσαγορεύω προσερῶ προσεῖπον προσερρήθην
= I exhort	παρακελεύομαι -σομαι -σάμην with dative
admiral	ναύαρχος -ου ὁ
admire, I	θαυμάζω*
advance, I	προχωρέω -ήσω προὐχώρησα

advantageous, it is ... to	συμφέρει with dative
adverse	ἐναντίος -α -ον
advise, I	παραινέω -έσω παρήνεσα with dative, πείθω*
Aegisthus	Αἴγισθος -ου ὁ
Aeneas	Αἰνείας -ου ὁ
Aeolis	Αἰολίς -ίδος ἡ
afraid, I am ... of	φοβέομαι*
after	μετά with accusative
again	αὖθις
Agamemnon	Ἀγαμέμνων -ονος ὁ
aid, I come to the ... of	βοηθέω -ήσω -ησα with dative
Alcibiades	Ἀλκιβιάδης -ου ὁ
Alcmaeon	Ἀλκμαίων -ωνος ὁ
alike	ὁμοίως
alive, I am	ζάω βιώσομαι ἐβίων
all	πᾶς πᾶσα πᾶν
all kinds of	παντοῖος -α -ον
alliance	συμμαχία -ας ἡ
allow, I	ἐάω*
ally	σύμμαχος -ου ὁ
along	κατά with accusative
already	ἤδη
also	καί
although	καίπερ with participle (see Chapter 17)
always	ἀεί
am, I	εἰμί*
ambassadors	πρέσβεις -εων οἱ
ambush	ἐνέδρα -ας ἡ
I set an ambush	ἐνέδραν ποιέομαι -ήσομαι -ησάμην
among	ἐν with dative
Amphion	Ἀμφίων -ονος ὁ
ancestor	πρόγονος -ου ὁ
and	καί
angry, I am, get ... (with)	ὀργίζομαι -ιοῦμαι ὠργίσθην (with dative)
animal	θηρίον -ου τό
announce	ἀγγέλλω*, ἐξαγγέλλω
annoy, I	λυπέω -ήσω -ησα -ήθην
answer, I	ἀποκρίνομαι*
Antony	Ἀντώνιος -ου ὁ
Apollo	Ἀπόλλων -ωνος ὁ

appeal to, please, I	ἀρέσκω ἀρέσω ἤρεσα with dative
appear, I	φαίνομαι* (see Chapter 17)
appoint, I	καθίστημι (see ἵστημι*)
approach, I	προσχωρέω -ήσω -ησα
appropriate, it is ... (for)	πρέπει (with dative)
archon	ἄρχων -οντος ὁ
Argos	Ἄργος -εος τό
arise, I (= happen)	γίγνομαι*
Armenians	Ἀρμένιοι -ων οἱ
arrest, I	συλλαμβάνω (see λαμβάνω*)
arrive, I	ἀφικνέομαι*
I have arrived	ἥκω -ξω (*impf.* ἧκον)
art	τέχνη -ης ἡ
as far as	ὅσον
as if	ὥσπερ with participle (see Chapter 17)
ask, I (a question)	ἐρωτάω*
= make a request	αἰτέω -ήσω -ησα -ήθην
assassin	σφαγεύς -εως ὁ
assembly	ἐκκλησία -ας ἡ
assert, I	διϊσχυρίζομαι -ιοῦμαι διϊσχυρισάμην
astonish, I	ἐκπλήσσω -ξω -ξα ἐξεπλάγην
Astura	Ἄστυρα -ων τά
Athenians	Ἀθηναῖοι -ων οἱ
Athens	Ἀθῆναι -ῶν αἱ
from Athens	Ἀθήνηθεν
in Athens	Ἀθήνησι(ν)
to Athens	Ἀθήναζε
attack	προσβολή -ῆς ἡ
attack, I	προσβάλλω (see βάλλω*) with dative, ἐπιτίθεμαι -θήσομαι -εθέμην with dative, ἐμπίπτω (see πίπτω*) with dative
attempt, I	πειράομαι*
attention, I pay	προσέχω (see ἔχω) τὸν νοῦν
Attica	Ἀττική -ῆς ἡ
audience	ἀκούοντες -ων οἱ
authorities, the	οἱ ἐν τέλει
Babylon	Βαβυλών -ῶνος ἡ
bad	κακός -ή -όν
banker	τραπεζίτης -ου ὁ

barbarians	βάρβαροι -ων οἱ
bat	νυκτερίς -ίδος ἡ
battle(field)	μάχη -ης ἡ
I join battle (with)	εἰς μάχην συνέρχομαι (see ἔρχομαι*) (with dative)
bay	κόλπος -ου ὁ
be, to	εἰμί*
beast, (wild)	θήριον -ου τό
beat, I	τύπτω -ψω -ψα -φθην
beautiful	καλός -ή -όν
very beautiful	κάλλιστος -η -ον
beauty	κάλλος -ους τό
because	ὅτι, διότι, ἅτε with participle (see Chapter 17)
become, I	γίγνομαι *
becomes, it	προσήκει with dative
before (*prep.*)	πρό with genitive
(*adv.*)	πρότερον, τὸ πρίν
(*conj.*)	πρίν (see Chapter 20)
beg, I	αἰτέω -ήσω -ησα -ήθην, παραιτέομαι -ήσομαι -ησάμην, ἀξιόω -ώσω -ωσα -ώθην, δέομαι δεήσομαι ἐδεήθην with genitive
beggar	πτωχός -οῦ ὁ
begin, I	ἄρχομαι*
believe, I	πιστεύω -σω -σα -θην with dative
belong to, I	προσήκω -ξω (*impf.*) προσῆκον
bequeath	καταλείπω (see λείπω*)
besiege, I	πολιορκέω -ήσω -ησα -ήθην
best	ἄριστος -η -ον
betray	προδίδωμι (see δίδωμι*)
better	ἀμείνων -ον, βελτίων -ον
bid, I	κελεύω -σω -σα -σθην
big	μέγας μεγάλη μέγα
bigger	μείζων -ον
biggest	μέγιστος -η -ον
birthday	γενέθλια -ων τά
bite, I	δάκνω δήξομαι ἔδακον ἐδήχθην
blameworthy, to blame	αἴτιος -α -ον
blessings	ἀγαθά -ῶν τά
board, I	ἐμβαίνω or εἰσβαίνω (see βαίνω*) εἰς with accusative

boat	πλοῖον -ου τό
body	σῶμα -ατος τό
= dead body, corpse	νεκρός -οῦ ὁ
bodyguard	δορυφόροι -ων οἱ
Boeotia	Βοιωτία -ας ἡ
book	βίβλος -ου ἡ
born, I am	γίγνομαι*
both	ἀμφότεροι -αι -α
both ... and	καί ... καί, τε ... καί
boy	παῖς παιδός ὁ
brave	ἀνδρεῖος -α -ον
bread	ἄρτος -ου ὁ
break, I	ῥήγνυμι ῥήξω ἔρρηξα ἐρράγην
(a line)	παραρρήγνυμι
(of a truce)	λύω -σω -σα -θην
(of laws = transgress)	παραβαίνω (see βαίνω*)
bribe	δῶρον -ου τό
bribe, I	διαφθείρω*, δώροις πείθω*
I am bribed	δωροδοκέω -ήσω -ησα
bridge	γέφυρα -ας ἡ
bring, I	φέρω*, κομίζω -ιῶ -σα -σθην
I bring down	καταφέρω
I bring up = rear	τρέφω θρέψω ἔθρεψα ἐτράφην
brother	ἀδελφός -οῦ ὁ
build, I	οἰκοδομέω -ήσω -ησα -ήθην
I am built round	περιβάλλομαι (see βάλλω) with dative
builder	οἰκοδόμος -ου ὁ
business	πράγματα -ων τά, ἐργασία -ας ἡ
but	ἀλλά, δέ (second word)
buy, I	ὠνέομαι -ήσομαι ἐπριάμην ἐωνήθην
by (means of)	διά with genitive
Byzantium	Βυζάντιον -ου τό
Cadmea	Καδμεία -ας ἡ
Cadmus	Κάδμος -ου ὁ
call, I	καλέω*
= I name	ὀνομάζω -σω -σα ⌐σθην
I call together	συγκαλέω (see καλέω*)
camp	στρατόπεδον -ου τό
captain	λοχαγός -οῦ ὁ

(of a ship)	ναύκληρος -ου ὁ, τριήραρχος -ου ὁ
capture	λαμβάνω*, αἱρέω*
I am captured	passive of above verbs, or ἁλίσκομαι ἁλώσομαι ἑάλων
care, I take	εὐλαβέομαι -ήσομαι -ήθην
carry, I	φέρω*, κομίζω -ιῶ -ισα -ίσθην
case = affairs, situation	πράγματα -ων τά
cavalryman	ἱππεύς -έως ὁ (*pl.* = cavalry)
cave	σπήλαιον -ου τό
cease, I ... (from)	παύομαι -σομαι -σάμην πέπαυμαι (with genitive), καταπαύομαι etc.
certain, a	τις τι
certainly	σαφῶς (δή)
chance, I	τύγχανω*
chase, I	διώκω*
cheer, I	θαρσύνω -υνῶ -υνα
chief men	πρῶτοι -ων οἱ
child	παῖς παιδός ὁ/ἡ, παίδιον -ου τό
choose, I	αἱρέομαι*
chop, I ... off	ἀποκόπτω (see κόπτω*)
Cicero	Κικέρων -ωνος ὁ
Cimon	Κίμων -ωνος ὁ
citadel	ἀκρόπολις -εως ἡ
Cithaeron	Κιθαιρών -ῶνος ὁ
citizen	πολίτης -ου ὁ
city	πόλις -εως ἡ
claim, I	φάσκω (only in present and imperfect)
clear	φανερός -ή -όν, δῆλος (-η) -ον
Clearchus	Κλέαρχος -ου ὁ
clever	δεινός -ή -όν
cling, I ... to	ἔχομαι (see ἔχω*) with genitive
close	συγκλείω -σω -σα -σθην (or συγκλῄω)
I close my eyes	συγκλῄω τά βλέφαρα
clothes, clothing	ἐσθής -ῆτος ἡ, σκευή -ῆς ἡ
Clytemnestra	Κλυταιμήστρα -ας ἡ
coast	παραλία -ας ἡ, ἀκτή -ῆς ἡ, or just say 'sea'
comb, I	κτενίζομαι
come, I	ἔρχομαι*
I have come	ἥκω -ξω (*impf.* ἧκον)
I come (against)	ἐπέρχομαι

I come forward	παρέρχομαι
I come in	εἰσέρχομαι
I come on = ensue	ἐπιγίγνομαι (see γίγνομαι*)
I come together	συνέρχομαι
command, I	κελεύω -σω -σα -σθην
command of, I am in	ἡγεμονεύω -σω -σα with genitive
commander	λοχαγός -οῦ ὁ
= commander-in-chief	στρατηγός -οῦ ὁ
compel, I	ἀναγκάζω -σω -σα -σθην
completely	παντάπασι(ν)
comrades (*voc.*)	ὦ ἄνδρες
conceal, I	κρύπτω -ψω -ψα -φθην
concerning	περί with genitive
concerns, it	μέλει with dative
condemn, I	καταγιγνώσκω (see γιγνώσκω*) with genitive of person and accusative of penalty
condition, in bad	φαῦλος -η -ον
condition that, on the	ἐφ' ᾧ or ἐφ' ᾧτε (see Chapter 15)
confident, I am	θαρρέω -ήσω -ησα
conquer, I	νικάω -ήσω -ησα -ήθην
conscious, I am	σύνοιδα (see οἶδα*) ἐμαυτῷ
consider, I (= think)	νομίζω*, ἡγέομαι -ήσομαι -ησάμην
conspiracy	συνωμοσία -ας ἡ
I form a conspiracy	συνωμοσίαν συνίστημι (see ἵστημι*)
constantly	ἀεί
consult (an oracle), I	χράομαι* with dative, μαντεύομαι -σομαι -ευσάμην
contest	ἀγών -ῶνος ὁ, ἅμιλλα -ης ἡ
= battle	μάχη -ης ἡ
continue, I	διατελέω -ῶ -εσα -έσθην (see Chapter 17)
Corcyraeans	Κερκυραῖοι -ων οἱ
Corinth	Κόρινθος -ου ἡ
Corinthians	Κορίνθιοι -ων οἱ
corrupt, I	διαφθείρω*
council	βουλή -ῆς ἡ
country	χώρα -ας ἡ
courage	ἀνδρεία -ας ἡ
I am of good courage	εὐθυμέω -ήσω -ησα
court (legal)	δικαστήριον -ου τό
to the court of	παρά with accusative

cowardice	δειλία -ας ἡ
criminal (*adj.*)	ἄδικος -ον
critical, at the ... moment	πρὸς καιρόν
Croesus	Κροῖσος -ου ὁ
cross, I (a river)	διαβαίνω (see βαίνω*)
(a mountain)	ὑπερβαίνω
crow	κόραξ -ακος ὁ
cuckoo	κόκκυξ -υγος ὁ
current	use present participle of πάρειμι
curtail, I	κατέχω (see ἔχω*)
cut down, I	κόπτω*
Cyclops	Κύκλωψ -ωπος ὁ
Cyprus	Κύπρος -ου ἡ
Cyprian	Κύπριος -α -ον
Cyrus	Κῦρος -ου ὁ
danger	κίνδυνος -ου ὁ
dangerous	χαλεπός -ή -όν
dare	τολμάω -ήσω -ησα -ήθην
Darius	Δαρεῖος -ου ὁ
dark	σκοτεινός -ή -όν
darkness	σκότος -ου ὁ
daughter	θυγάτηρ -τρός ἡ
dawn	ἕως -ω ἡ
at dawn	ἅμα τῇ ἕῳ, ἅμα τῇ ἡμέρᾳ
day	ἡμέρα -ας ἡ
every day	καθ’ (ἑκάστην τὴν) ἡμέραν
the next day	ὑστεραία -ας ἡ
days, in the ... of	ἐπί with genitive
deaf and dumb	κωφός -ή -όν
death	θάνατος -ου ὁ
I put to death	ἀποκτείνω* (*pass.* ἀποθνῄσκω*)
deceive, I	ἀπατάω -ήσω -ησα -ήθην, ἐξαπατάω etc.
decide	βουλεύομαι -σομαι -σάμην, or use impersonal δοκεῖ (δόξει ἔδοξε) with dative and infinitive
deep	βαθύς -εῖα -ύ
defeat, I	νικάω -ήσω -ησα -ήθην
defend, I	ἀμύνω -υνῶ ἤμυνα with dative, φυλάσσω*
= I speak in my own defence	ἀπολογέομαι -ήσομαι -ησάμην

deliberately	ἐπιτηδές
deliver, I	διασῴζω (see σῴζω*)
Delphi	Δελφοί -ῶν οἱ
Demosthenes	Δημοσθένης -ους ὁ
deny, I	ἀπαρνέομαι -ήσομαι ἀπηρνήθην (see Chapter 18)
depart, I	ἀπέρχομαι (see ἔρχομαι*)
deprive, I	στερέω -ήσω -ησα -ήθην
deserter	αὐτόμολος -ου ὁ
deserving (of)	ἄξιος -α -ον (with genitive)
desire, I	ἐπιθυμέω -ήσω -ησα with genitive or infinitive
despair	ἀθυμία -ας ἡ
despair, I	ἀθυμέω -ήσω -ησα, ἀθυμῶς ἔχω*
despatch, I	ἀποπέμπω*, ἀποστέλλω*
despise, I	ὀλιγωρέω -ήσω -ησα with genitive, καταφρονέω -ήσω -ησα with genitive
destroy, I	διαφθείρω*, ἀπόλλυμι*
detachment	λόχος -ου ὁ
determine, I	βουλεύομαι -σομαι -σάμην, or use impersonal δοκεῖ (δόξει ἔδοξε) with dative and infinitive
devise, I	μηχανάομαι -ήσομαι -ησάμην
die, I	ἀποθνῄσκω*
difficult	χαλεπός -ή -όν
difficulty (*or pl.*)	ἀπορία -ας ἡ
I am in difficulties	ἐν ἀπορίᾳ εἰμί, ἀπορέω -ήσω -ησα
din	θόρυβος -ου ὁ
I raise a din	θορυβέω -ήσω -ησα
dine, I	δειπνέω -ήσω -ησα
dinner	δεῖπνον -ου τό
disaster	συμφορά -ᾶς ἡ
disbelieve, I	ἀπιστέω -ήσω -ησα -ήθην with dative
disclose, I	ἀποφαίνω (see φαίνω*)
discover, I	γιγνώσκω*, πυνθάνομαι*
disembark, I	ἐκβαίνω (see βαίνω*) ἐκ with genitive
disgraceful	αἰσχρός -ά -όν
disheartened, I am	ἀθυμέω -ήσω -ησα
dispirited, I am	ἀθυμέω -ήσω -ησα
displeased at, I am	χαλεπῶς φέρω*
distant, I am	ἀπέχω (see ἔχω*)
do, I	ποιέω -ήσω -ησα -ήθην

doctor	ἰατρός -οῦ ὁ
dog	κύων κυνός ὁ
Dolonci	Δόλογκοι -ων οἱ
dominion, under the..of	ὑποχείριος -ον with dative
door	θύρα -ας ἡ
drag	ἕλκω*
I drag down	καθέλκω (see ἕλκω*)
draw up, I	τάττω*
dream	ἐνύπνιον -ου τό
dress in, I	ἐνδύομαι -σομαι -σάμην
drink	ποτός -οῦ ὁ
drink, I	πίνω*
dumb	ἄφωνος -ον
dungeon	δεσμωτήριον -ου τό
each	ἕκαστος -η -ον
on each occasion	ἑκάστοτε
easy	ῥᾴδιος -α -ον
easiest	ῥᾷστος -η -ον
eat, I	ἐσθίω ἔδομαι ἔφαγον ἠδέσθην
educate, I	παιδεύω -σω -σα -θην
Egyptian	Αἰγύπτιος -α -ον
eight	ὀκτώ
either ... or	ἤ ... ἤ
elders	πρεσβύτεροι -ων οἱ (with or without ἄνδρες)
Electra	Ἠλέκτρα -ας ἡ
embark	ἐμβαίνω (see βαίνω*) εἰς with accusative
empire	ἀρχή -ῆς ἡ
empty	κενός -ή -όν
encamp, I	στρατοπεδεύομαι -σομαι -σάμην, αὐλίζομαι (*aor.* ηὐλισάμην)
encourage	παραμυθέομαι -ήσομαι -ησάμην with dative
endure, I	φέρω*
= I suffer	πάσχω*
enemy	πολέμιοι -ων οἱ
= personal enemy	ἐχθρός -οῦ ὁ
enraged, I am	ὀργίζομαι -ιοῦμαι ὠργίσθην
enslave, I	δουλόω -ώσω -ωσα -ώθην
entertain, I	ξενίζω -ιῶ -ισα -ίσθην
entertainment	ξένια -ων τά

envoys	πρεσβεῖς -εων οἱ
ephor	ἔφορος -ου ὁ
escape, I	ἐκφεύγω (see φεύγω*)
estimation, I form an	διαγιγνώσκω (see γιγνώσκω*)
Euboea	Εὔβοια -ας ἡ
even	καί, ἔτι
Evenus	Εὔηνος -ου ὁ
everyone, everything	πάντες πάντα
everywhere	πανταχοῦ
evil	κακός -ή -όν, πονηρός -ή -όν
excessively, to excess	περισσῶς
exhort, I	παρακελεύομαι -σομαι -σάμην with dative
exile	
= person	φυγάς -άδος ὁ
= banishment	φυγή -ῆς ἡ
expedition	στρατεία -ας ἡ
= naval expedition	ἔκπλους -οῦ ὁ
explain, I	ἐξηγέομαι -ήσομαι -ησαμήν, διηγέομαι etc, διεξηγέομαι
eye	ὄφθαλμος -ου ὁ
fall, I	πίπτω*
I fall upon	προσπίπτω with dative, ἐμπίπτω with dative
famous	γνώριμος -η -ον, κλεινός -ή -όν
farmer	αὐτουργός -οῦ ὁ
father	πατήρ πατρός ὁ
favour, I do a	χαρίζομαι -ιοῦμαι -ισάμην with dative
fear	φόβος -ου ὁ
fear, I	φοβέομαι*
fearlessly, without fear	ἀφόβως
festivity (*or pl.*)	εὐφροσύνη -ης ἡ
few	ὀλίγοι -αι -α
field	ἀγρός -οῦ ὁ
fifty	πεντήκοντα
fight, I (with/against)	μάχομαι* (with dative)
finally	τέλος
find, I	εὑρίσκω*
= I come upon, catch	καταλαμβάνω (see λαμβάνω*)
I find out	πυνθάνομαι*
fine	καλός -ή -όν

first	πρῶτος -η -ον
at first	πρῶτον
I am the first to	use φθάνω with participle (see Chapter 17)
fitting, it is	πρέπει with dative
flank	κέρας -ατος τό
on the flank	κατὰ κέρας
flee, I	φεύγω*
I flee away	ἀποφεύγω (see φεύγω*)
fleet	ναυτικόν -οῦ τό
flight	φυγή -ῆς ἡ
I put to flight	εἰς φυγὴν καθίστημι (see ἵστημι*), τρέπω*
I take to flight	εἰς φυγὴν καθίσταμαι
flower	ἄνθος -ους τό
flute-girl	αὐλητρίς -ίδος ἡ
fly up, I	προσπέτομαι -πτήσομαι -επτάμην
follow, I	ἕπομαι*
= I pursue	διωκω*
fond, I am ... of	ἀγαπάω -ήσω -ησα
food	σῖτος -ου ὁ
foolish	μῶρος -α -ον
foot	πούς ποδός ὁ
for	γάρ (second word)
forbid, I	οὐκ ἐάω*, ἀπαγορεύω -σω ἀπεῖπον with dative
force (= army)	στρατός -οῦ ὁ, στρατιά -ᾶς ἡ, στράτευμα -ατος τό
ford	πόρος -ου ὁ
foreign	βάρβαρος -ον
foreign parts	ἡ βάρβαρος (sc. χώρα)
forest	ὕλη -ης ἡ
forgive, I	συγγιγνώσκω (see γιγνώσκω*) with dative
fort	τείχισμα -ατος τό
fortify, I	(περι)τειχίζω -ιῶ -ισα -ίσθην
fortunate	εὐτυχής -ές
forty	τετταράκοντα
four	τέσσαρες τέσσαρα
fourth	τέταρτος -η -ον
frequently	πολλάκις
friend	φίλος -ου ὁ
friendly	φίλιος -α -ον
I am on ... terms with	φιλίως ἔχω* with dative

frightening	φοβερός -ά -όν
from	ἀπό with genitive
(*a person*)	παρά with genitive
front, in	(ἐκ τοῦ) ἔμπροσθεν
fruit	καρπός -οῦ ὁ
fugitive	φεύγων -οντος ὁ
full	πλήρης -ες
furiously	προπετῶς
future, in the	τοῦ λοιποῦ
garden	κῆπος -ου ὁ
gate	πύλη -ης ἡ
gather, I	συλλέγω -ξω -ξα -χθην
general	στρατηγός -οῦ ὁ
I am general	στρατηγέω -ήσω -ησα
gentleman	καλὸς κἀγαθός ὁ
get away, I	ἀπέρχομαι (see ἔρχομαι*)
I get back to	ἐπανέρχομαι
I get hold of	λαμβάνομαι (see λαμβάνω*) with genitive
I get to	use ἀφικνέομαι* εἰς with accusative
giant	γίγας -αντος ὁ
gift	δῶρον -ου τό
girl	παῖς παιδός ἡ, κόρη -ης ἡ
girlfriend	φίλη -ης ἡ
give, I	δίδωμι*
I give away	ἀποδίδωμι
I give back	ἀποδίδωμι
I give in (= surrender)	ἐνδίδωμι
gladly	ἡδέως, ἀσμένως
go, I	ἔρχομαι*
I go about, to and fro	φοιτάω -ήσω -ησα
I go around	περιέρχομαι
I go away, go off	ἀπέρχομαι
I go forward	προχωρέω -ήσω προὔχωρησα
I go into	εἰσέρχομαι
I go on board, embark	ἐμβαίνω (see βαίνω*) εἰς with accusative
I go out	ἐξέρχομαι, ἐκβαίνω
I go over to	μεθίσταμαι (see ἵστημι*) παρά with accusative
I go to	προσέρχομαι
god	θεός -οῦ ὁ

goddess	θεά -ᾶς ἡ
going to, I am	μέλλω* with infinitive (usually future)
gold	χρυσός -οῦ ὁ
good	ἀγαθός -ή -όν
government	οἱ ἄρχοντες, οἱ ἐν τέλει
governor	use ἄρχων -οντος ὁ
grandfather	πάππος -ου ὁ
grateful, I am ... to	χάριν οἶδα* with dative
gratify, I	χαρίζομαι -ιοῦμαι -ισάμην with dative
great	μέγας μεγάλη μέγα
Greece	Ἑλλας -άδος ἡ
greedy for gain	αἰσχροκερδής -ές
Greeks	Ἕλληνες -ων οἱ
greet, I	δέχομαι*
groan, I	στένω (only in pres. and impf.), ἀποιμώζω -ξομαι -ξα
ground	πέδον -ου τό, γῆ γῆς ἡ
on the ground	χαμαί
grounds, on the ... that	ὡς with participle (see Chapter 17)
guard, I	φυλάττω or φυλάσσω*
I am on my guard	φυλάττομαι or φυλάσσομαι
guest	ξένος -ου ὁ
guilty (of)	αἴτιος -α -ον (with genitive)
Gylippus	Γύλιππος -ου ὁ
hair	κόμαι -ῶν αἱ
hand	χείρ -ός ἡ
hand over, I	παραδίδωμι (see δίδωμι*)
handicraft	χειρούργημα -ατος τό
hand-to-hand combat,	
I engage in	εἰς χεῖρας συνέρχομαι (see ἔρχομαι*)
happen, I	τυγχάνω* with participle (see Chapter 17)
= I take place	γίγνομαι*
happy	εὐδαίμων -ον
harbour	λιμήν -ένος ὁ
hardly	μόλις
hardship	πόνος -ου ὁ, or use n. pl. of δεινός or κακός
harm	βλάβη -ης ἡ, κακόν -οῦ τό
hate, I	μισέω -ήσω -ησα -ήθην
have, I	ἔχω*

have to, I	use δεῖ or χρή with accusative
head	κεφαλή -ῆς ἡ
hear	ἀκούω* with accusative of thing (i.e. the sound), but genitive of person (i.e. the source of the sound)
Hector	Ἕκτωρ -ορος ὁ
help, I	ὠφελέω -ήσω -ησα -ήθην
I come to help	βοηθέω -ήσω -ησα with dative
herald	κῆρυξ -υκος ὁ
herdsman	βουκόλος -ου ὁ
here	ἐνθάδε
to here, hither	δεῦρο
from here	ἐνθένδε
I am here	πάρειμι (see εἰμί*)
Herennius	Ἑρέννιος -ου ὁ
Hermocrates	Ἑρμοκράτης -ου ὁ
hide, I	κρύπτω -ψω -ψα -φθην
high	ὑψηλός -ή -όν
hill	λόφος -ου ὁ
hold, I	ἔχω*
home	οἶκος -ου ὁ
home(wards)	οἴκαδε, ἐπ᾽ οἴκου
at home	οἴκοι
I am away from home	ἀποδημέω -ήσω -ησα
Homer	Ὅμηρος -ου ὁ
honour	τιμή -ῆς ἡ
honour, I	τιμάω -ήσω -ησα -ήθην
honourable	χρηστός -ή -όν
hope, I	ἐλπίζω*
hopeless, I am	ἀνελπίστως ἔχω*
hoplite	ὁπλίτης -ου ὁ
horse	ἵππος -ου ὁ
host, great host	πλῆθος -ους τό
hostage	ὅμηρος -ου ὁ
hot	θερμός -ή -όν
hour	ὥρα -ας ἡ
house	οἰκία -ας ἡ
how big ?	πόσος -η -ον ;
how many ?	πόσοι -αι -α ;
however	μέντοι (second word)
huge	μεγας μεγάλη μέγα

hundred	ἑκατόν
hunger	λιμός -οῦ ὁ
hunt, go hunting, I	θηρεύω -σω -σα -θην
hurry, I	ἐπείγομαι -ξομαι -χθην
husband	ἀνήρ ἀνδρός ὁ
I	ἐγώ
ignorance	ἄγνοια -ας ἡ
ignorant	ἀμαθής -ές
I am ignorant	ἀγνοέω -ήσω -ησα
ill, I am	νοσέω -ήσω -ησα
illness	νόσος -ου ἡ
imagine, I	νομίζω*
immediately	εὐθύς
immortal	ἀθάνατος -ον
impious	ἀσεβής -ές
implore, I	αἰτέω -ήσω -ησα -ήθην, παραιτέομαι -ήσομαι -ησάμην, ἀξιόω -ώσω -ωσα -ώθην, δέομαι δεήσομαι ἐδεήθην with genitive
imprison, I	καθείργω -ξω -ξα -χθην
in	ἐν with dative
inactive, I remain	ἡσυχάζω -σω -σα
increase, I	αὐξάνω αὐξήσω ηὔξησα ηὐξήθην
indeed	δή
and indeed	καὶ δὴ καί
infantryman	πεζός -οῦ ὁ (*pl.*= infantry)
inform, I	λεγω*, ἀγγέλλω*
inhabitants	ἔνοικοι -ων οἱ, ἐνοικοῦντες -ων οἱ
injustice	ἀδικία -ας ἡ
I do an injustice	ἀδικέω -ήσω -ησα -ήθην
instruction	πρόσταγμα -ατος τό
intend, I	ἐν νῷ ἔχω*, μέλλω* (usually future infin. after μέλλω)
intentionally	ἑκών -οῦσα -όν
interest, it is in the ... of	συμφέρει with dative, λυσιτελεῖ with dative
into	εἰς with accusative
invade, I	εἰσβάλλω (see βάλλω*) εἰς with accusative
invite, I	καλέω*
irritated, I am ... (with)	ἀγανακτέω -ήσω -ησα (with dative)
island	νῆσος -ου ἡ

islander	νησιώτης -ου ὁ
Italy	Ἰταλία -ας ἡ
journey	πορεία -ας ἡ, ὁδός -οῦ ἡ
journey, I	πορεύομαι -σομαι -σάμην or -θην, ὁδοιπορέω -ήσω ὡδοιπόρησα
judge	κριτής -οῦ ὁ
juror	δικαστής -οῦ ὁ
just	δίκαιος -α -ον
keep, I	ἔχω*
I keep hold of	κατέχω (see ἔχω*)
kill, I	ἀποκτείνω*
I am killed	ἀποθνήσκω*
kindly	εὐμενῶς, ἠπίως
king	βασιλεύς -έως ὁ
I am king	βασιλεύω -σω -σα
know, I	οἶδα*
I don't know	ἀγνοέω -ήσω -ησα -ήθην
I get to know	γιγνώσκω*, πυνθάνομαι*
labour	πόνος -ου ὁ
Lacedaemonians	Λακεδαιμόνιοι -ων οἱ
lack, am short of, I	σπανίζω -ιῶ -ισα with genitive
Laconia	Λακωνική -ῆς ἡ
lad	μειράκιον -ου τό
land	γῆ -ῆς ἡ, ἀγροί -ῶν οἱ
by land	κατὰ γῆν
language	γλῶσσα -ης ἡ
last, at	τέλος
later	ὕστερον
law	νόμος -ου ὁ
I go to law	εἰς κρίσιν ἔρχομαι*
lazy	ῥάθυμος -ον
lead, I	ἄγω*
I lead away	ἀπάγω
I lead out	ἐξάγω
leader	ἡγεμών -όνος ὁ, ἄρχων -οντος ὁ
learn	μανθάνω*
leave (= leave behind)	λείπω*, καταλείπω

(= depart from)	ἐξέρχομαι (see ἔρχομαι*) ἐκ with genitive or ἀπέρχομαι ἀπό with genitive
left (hand etc.)	ἀριστερός -ά -όν
length	μῆκος -ους τό
lesser	ἐλάσσων -ον
let go, I	ἀφίημι (see ἵημι*)
letter	ἐπιστολή -ῆς ἡ
lie, I	κεῖμαι κείσομαι (*impf.* ἐκείμην)
= I am untruthful	ψεύδομαι -σομαι -σάμην
like, I	φιλέω -ήσω -ησα -ήθην
likely to, I am	μέλλω*
listen to, I	ἀκροάομαι -άσομαι -ασάμην with genitive of person, ἀκούω* with genitive of person
litter	φορεῖον -ου τό
live, I	
= am alive	ζάω βιώσομαι ἐβίων
= dwell	οἰκέω -ήσω ᾤκησα ᾠκήθην
= dwell in	ἐνοικέω etc. ἐν with dative
= pass the time	διάγω (see ἄγω*)
local	ἐγχώριος (-α) -ον
lock, I	κλείω -σω -σα -σθην (or κλῄω)
London	Λονδίνη -ης ἡ
long	μακρός -ά -όν
look at, I	βλέπω -ψομαι -ψα εἰς with accusative
lose, I	ἀπόλλυμι*, ἀποβάλλω (see βάλλω*)
I lose my way	ἁμαρτάνω* τῆς ὁδοῦ
loss, I am at a ... (for)	ἀπορέω -ήσω -ησα (with genitive)
love	φιλέω -ήσω -ησα -ήθην
Lydians	Λυδοί -ῶν οἱ
Macedonia	Μακεδονία -ας ἡ
madness	ἄτη -ης ἡ
majority	πολλοί -ῶν οἱ
make, I	ποιέω -ήσω -σα -θην
I make known	ἀποδείκνυμι (see δείκνυμι*)
I make my way	πορεύομαι -σομαι -σάμην or -θην
man	ἀνήρ ἀνδρός ὁ
= human being	ἄνθρωπος -ου ὁ
Mania	Μανία -ας ἡ
many	πολλοί -αί -ά

Vocabulary

Marathon	Μαραθών -ῶνος ὁ
at Marathon	Μαραθῶνι
march, I	πορεύομαι -σομαι -σάμην or -θην, στρατεύω -σω -σα
day's march	σταθμός -οῦ ὁ
marine	ἐπιβάτης -ου ὁ
market-place	ἀγορά -ᾶς ἡ
marriage	γάμος -ου ὁ
marry, I (of a man)	γαμέω γαμῶ ἔγημα ἐγαμήθην
(of a woman)	γαμέομαι γαμοῦμαι ἐγημάμην with dative
master	δεσπότης -ου ὁ
matter	πρᾶγμα -ατος τό
meal	δεῖπνον -ου τό
I have a meal	δειπνέω -ήσω -ησα
means, by no	οὐδαμῶς
meet, I	ἐντυγχάνω (see τυγχάνω*) with dative
I go to meet	ἀπαντάω -ήσω -ησα with dative
merchant	ἔμπορος -ου ὁ
messenger	ἄγγελος -ου ὁ
middle	μέσος -η -ον
Midias	Μειδίας -ου ὁ
Miltiades	Μιλτιάδης -ου ὁ
mindful (of)	μνήμων -ον (with genitive)
mistaken, I am	ἁμαρτάνω*
mob	πλῆθος -ους τό, ὄχλος -ου ὁ
money	χρήματα -ων τά, ἀργύριον -ου τό
month	μήν μηνός ὁ
moon	σελήνη -ης ἡ
more (adj.)	πλείων πλεῖον
(adv.)	μᾶλλον
mother	μήτηρ -τρός ἡ
mother-in-law	ἑκυρά -ᾶς ἡ
mountain	ὄρος -ους τό
murder	φόνος -ου ὁ
murder, I	φονεύω -σω -σα -θην
murderer	φονεύς -έως ὁ, σφαγεύς -έως ὁ
music	μουσική -ῆς ἡ
must	use the impersonals δεῖ or χρή (both with accusative)
my	ἐμός ἐμή ἐμόν

Mytilene	Μυτιλήνη -ης ἡ
name	ὄνομα -ατος τό
native	ἐπιχώριος (-α) -ον
native land	πατρίς -ίδος ἡ
navy	ναυτικόν -οῦ τό
near	ἐγγύς with genitive
necessary, it is	δεῖ* with accusative, χρή* with accusative
what is necessary	τὰ δέοντα
necessity	ἀνάγκη -ης ἡ
neck	τράχηλος -ου ὁ
need, I	δέομαι δεήσομαι ἐδεήθην with genitive
neglect, I	ὀλιγωρέω -ήσω -ησα -ήθην with genitive
neighbour	γείτων -ονος ὁ
never	οὐδέποτε, οὔποτε, μηδέποτε, μήποτε (see Appendix 3)
nevertheless	ὅμως
new	νέος -α -ον
Nicias	Νικίας -ου ὁ
night(fall)	νύξ νυκτός ἡ
nine	ἐννέα
ninth	ἔνατος -η -ον
no longer	οὐκέτι, μηκέτι (see Appendix 3)
no one, nothing	οὐδείς οὐδέν, μηδείς μηδέν (see Appendix 3)
noble	εὐγενής -ές, γενναῖος -α ον
nonetheless	ὅμως
nonsense, I talk	φλυαρέω -ήσω -ησα
not	οὐ, μή (see Appendix 3)
not at all	οὐδαμῶς, μηδαμῶς (see Appendix 3)
notice, I	αἰσθάνομαι*
now	νῦν
= by now, already	ἤδη
obey, I	πείθομαι* with dative
Odysseus	Ὀδυσσεύς -έως ὁ
Oedipus	Οἰδίπους -ποδος ὁ
offering	ἀνάθημα -ατος τό
officer	λοχαγός -οῦ ὁ
often	πολλάκις
old	ἀρχαῖος -α -ον, παλαιός -ά -όν

old man	γέρων -οντος ὁ
of old	πάλαι
omen	σημεῖον -ου τό
on	ἐν with dative, ἐπί with genitive
once, at one time	ποτέ
at once, immediately	εὐθύς, παραυτίκα
one	εἷς μία ἕν
only	μόνον
not only ... but also	οὐ μόνον ... ἀλλὰ καί
open, in the ... (air)	ἐν ὑπαίθρῳ
open, I	ἀνοίγνυμι ἀνοίξω ἀνέῳξα ἀνεῴχθην
opponent	ἐναντίος -ου ὁ
opportunity	καιρός -οῦ ὁ
oppose, I	ἀνθίσταμαι ἀντιστήσομαι ἀντέστην with dative
oracle	χρήστηριον -ου τό
orator	ῥήτωρ -ορος ὁ
order, I	κελεύω -σω -σα -σθην
Orestes	Ὀρέστης -ου ὁ
our	ἡμέτερος -α -ον
out of	ἐκ with genitive
overjoyed, I am	ὑπερήδομαι -ησθήσομαι -ήσθην
overtake, I	καταλαμβάνω (see λαμβάνω*)
owe, I	ὀφείλω -ήσω ὤφελον
ox	βοῦς βοός ὁ/ἡ
panic	ἔκπληξις -εως ἡ
parent	γονεύς -έως ὁ
part	μέρος -ους τό
for my part	τὸ ἐπ' ἐμέ
I have a part in	μέτεστι (see Chapter 21)
pass	πάροδος -ου ἡ
pass, I ... through	διαβαίνω (see βαίνω*)
= I survive, surmount	περιγίγνομαι (see γίγνομαι*) with genitive
patriotic	φιλόπατρις -ιδος
Pausanias	Παυσανίας -ου ὁ
pay, I ... attention	προσέχω (see ἔχω*) τὸν νοῦν
penalty	ζημία -ας ἡ
I pay the penalty	δίκην or δίκας δίδωμι*
Penelope	Πηνελόπη -ης ἡ

people = persons	ἄνθρωποι -ων οἱ
= nation	ἔθνος -ους τό
= common people	δῆμος -ου ὁ
perceive, I	αἰσθάνομαι*
perfectly well	σαφῶς
perhaps	ἴσως
perish, I	ἀπόλλυμαι (see ἀπόλλυμι*)
permitted (to), it is	ἔξεστι or πάρεστι (with dative)
Persia	Περσική -ῆς ἡ
Persians	Πέρσαι -ῶν οἱ, Μῆδοι -ων οἱ
persuade	πείθω*
Pharnabazus	Φαρνάβαζος -ου ὁ
Phidippides	Φειδιππίδης -ου ὁ
Philip	Φίλιππος -ου ὁ
philosopher	φιλόσοφος -ου ὁ
Phocian	Φωκεύς -έως ὁ
Phocis	Φωκίς -ίδος ἡ
Pisistratus	Πεισίστρατος -ου ὁ
place	χωρίον -ου τό
plan	βουλή -ῆς ἡ
Plataea	Πλαταιαί -ῶν αἱ
Plataeans	Πλαταιῆς -έων οἱ
play, I	παίζω παιξοῦμαι ἔπαισα
please, I	ἀρέσκω ἀρέσω ἤρεσα with dative
pleased, I am	ἥδομαι ἡσθήσομαι ἤσθην
pleasure	ἡδονή -ῆς ἡ
with pleasure	καθ’ ἡδονήν
plot, I ... against	ἐπιβουλεύω -σω -σα -θην with dative
poem	ποίημα -ατος τό
poet	ποιητής -οῦ ὁ
policeman	use τοξότης -ου ὁ
politician	ῥήτωρ -ορος ὁ
Polybus	Πόλυβος -ου ὁ
Polyphemus	Πολύφημος -ου ὁ
poor	πένης -ητος
Popillius	Ποπίλλιος -ου ὁ
position (military)	χωρίον -ου τό
I take up a position	καθίσταμαι καταστήσομαι κατέστην
possessions	κτήματα -ων τά
possible (for), it is	ἔξεστι or πάρεστι (with dative)

praise, I	ἐπαινέω*
pray, I (to)	εὔχομαι -ξομαι -ξάμην
present, I am	πάρειμι (see εἰμί*)
prepare, I	παρασκευάζω -σω παρεσκεύασα παρεσκευάσθην
preserve, I	σώζω*
press hard, I	πιέζω -σω -σα -σθην
pretend, I	προσποιέομαι -ήσομαι -ησάμην
prevent, I	κωλύω -σω -σα -θην, εἴργω εἴρξω εἶρξα εἴρχθην (see Chapter 18)
previously	πρότερον
Priam	Πρίαμος -ου ὁ
priest	ἱερεύς -έως ὁ
prison	δεσμωτήριον -ου τό
prisoner	δεσμώτης -ου ὁ
(of war)	αἰχμάλωτος, -ου ὁ
I take prisoner	ζωγρέω -ήσω -ησα -ήθην
prize	ἆθλον -ου τό
probably	εἰκότως, κατὰ τὸ εἰκός
promise, I	ὑπισχνέομαι*
proposal	λόγος -ου ὁ
propose to, I	παραινέω -έσω παρήνεσα with dative, πείθω*
provide, I	παρέχω (see ἔχω*)
provisions	ἐπιτήδεια -ων τά
public	κοινός -ή -όν, δημόσιος -α -ον
at public expense	δημοσίᾳ
public treasury	κοινόν -οῦ τό
punish, I	κολάζω -σω -σα -σθην, δίκην λαμβάνω* παρά with genitive
I am punished	either passive of κολάζω or δίκας δίδωμι*
punishment	ζημία -ας ἡ
pupil	μαθητής -οῦ ὁ
pursue, I	διώκω*
put in to, I (of ships)	προσέχω (see ἔχω*) εἰς with accusative
I put back to shore	κατάγομαι -ξομαι κατηγαγόμην
I put out to sea	ἀνάγομαι -ξομαι ἀνηγαγόμην
Pylades	Πυλάδης -ου ὁ
Pylos	Πύλος -ου ἡ
Pythia	Πυθία -ας ἡ

quarry, I	τέμνω*
queen	βασίλεια -ας ἡ
quick	ταχύς -εῖα -ύ
quiet, I am	σιγάω -ήσομαι -ησα -ήθην
rains, it	ὕει ὕσει ὕσει(ν)
reach, I	ἀφικνέομαι* εἰς with accusative
read, I	ἀναγιγνώσκω (see γιγνώσκω*)
ready	ἑτοῖμος (-η) -ον
realise, I	γιγνώσκω*, αἰσθάνομαι*
reality, in	τῷ ὄντι
rebuild, I	ἀνοικοδομέω -ήσω -ησα -ήθην
receive, I	δέχομαι*
refuge, I take ... in	καταφεύγω (see φεύγω*) εἰς with accusative
refuse, I	οὐκ ἐθέλω*
reinforcements	βοηθοί -ῶν οἱ
rejoice, I	χαίρω χαιρήσω ἐχάρην
relatives	συγγενεῖς -ῶν οἱ
release, I	λύω -σω -σα -θην, ἐλευθερόω -ώσω -ωσα -ώθην
reliable	πιστός -ή -όν
remain, I	μένω*
I remain in	ἐμμένω (see μένω*)
remember, I	μέμνημαι μνησθήσομαι ἐμνήσθην with genitive, or use μνήμων with εἶναι
remind, I	ἀναμιμνήσκω ἀναμνήσω ἀνέμνησα ἀνεμνήσθην
reply	ἀποκρίνομαι*
report	use λόγοι -ων οἱ
representatives	πρέσβεις -εων οἱ
reputation	δόξα -ης ἡ
resist, I	ἀμύνομαι -οῦμαι -άμην, ἀνθίσταμαι (see ἵστημι*) with dative
resolve, I	βουλεύομαι -σομαι -σάμην, or use impersonal δοκεῖ (δόξει, ἔδοξε) with dative and infinitive
respite	ἀνάπαυλα -ης ἡ (or pl.)
responsible (for)	αἴτιος -α -ον (with genitive)
rest, the	ἄλλοι -ων οἱ
rest of, the	use ἄλλος -η -ο
result, as a	ὥστε

retreat, I	ἀναχωρέω -ήσω -ησα
return, I	ἐπανέρχομαι (see ἔρχομαι*)
(from exile)	κατέρχομαι
reveal, I	ἀποφαίνω (see φαίνω*), ἐκφαίνω, μηνύω -σω -σα -θην, δηλόω -ώσω -ωσα -ώθην
reward, I	χάριν ἀποδίδωμι (see δίδωμι*) with dative
rich	πλούσιος -α -ον
right (hand etc.)	δεξιός -ά -όν
rightly	ὀρθῶς
rise, I (of the sun)	ἀνατέλλω (*aor.*) -έτειλα
risk, I run the ... of	κινδυνεύω -σω -σα with infinitive
river	ποταμός -οῦ ὁ
road	ὁδός -οῦ ἡ
Rome	Ῥώμη -ης ἡ
room	οἴκημα -ατος τό
rule, I	ἄρχω*
ruler	ἄρχων -οντος ὁ
run, I	τρέχω*
I run away, flee	φεύγω*
I run out	ἐκτρέχω
sacrosanct	ἄσυλος -ον
sail, I	πλέω*
I sail away	ἀποπλέω
sailor	ναύτης -ου ὁ
same, the	ὁ αὐτός etc.
at the same time (as)	ἅμα (with dative)
sand	ψάμμος -ου ἡ
Sardis	Σάρδεις -εων αἱ
satisfy, I	ἀρέσκω ἀρέσω ἤρεσα with dative
satrap	σατράπης -ου ὁ
satrapy	σατραπεία -ας ἡ
save, I	σῴζω*
say	λέγω*, φημί*
scarcely	μόλις
scatter, I	διασκεδάννυμι -σκεδῶ -εσκέδασα -εσκεδάσθην
school	διδασκαλεῖον -ου τό
scorn, I	ὀλιγωρέω -ήσω -ησα -ήθην with genitive
scout	κατάσκοπος -ου ὁ

screech, I	κλάζω -γξω -γξα
sea	θάλασσα -ης ἡ (or θάλαττα)
by sea	κατὰ θάλατταν
sea battle	ναυμαχία -ας ἡ
search, I ... (for)	ζητέω -ήσω -ησα -ήθην
secret	ἀπόρρητον -ου τό
secretly	λάθρᾳ
see, I	ὁράω*
seek, I ... (after)	ζητέω -ήσω -ησα -ήθην
seize, I	λαμβάνω*
-self	αὐτός -ή -ό
sell, I	πωλέω -ήσω -ησα, ἀποδίδομαι -δώσομαι -εδόμην
senate	βουλή -ῆς
send, I	πέμπω*
I send back	ἀποπέμπω
I send for	μεταπέμπομαι
sensible	φρόνιμος -ον
serious	μέγας μεγάλη μέγα
seriously	μάλιστα, σφόδρα
serve, I	ὑπηρετέω -ήσω -ησα with dative
service, I do a	ὠφελέω, -ήσω, -ησα, -ήθην
set down, I	κατατίθημι (see τίθημι*)
set out, I	ἀφορμάομαι -ηθήσομαι -ήθην, πορεύομαι -σομαι -σάμην or -θην, αἴρω*
settle, I	καθίζω*
share in, I	μετέχω (see ἔχω*) with genitive
shepherd	ποιμήν -ένος ὁ
shield	ἀσπίς -ίδος ἡ
ship	ναῦς νεώς ἡ
shore	use γῆ γῆς ἡ
short of, I am	σπανίζω -ιῶ -ισα with genitive
shout	βοή -ῆς ἡ
shout, I	βοάω -ήσομαι -ησα
show myself, I	φαίνομαι* (see Chapter 17)
shudder, I ... at	ἀποκνέω -ήσω -ησα
Sicilians	Σίκελοι -ων οἱ
Sicily	Σικελία -ας ἡ
side, on the ... of	μετά with genitive
I fight on the side of	συμμάχομαι (see μάχομαι*) with dative

165

sight of, I catch	καθοράω (see ὁράω*)
silent, I am	σιγάω -ήσομαι -ησα -ήθην
since (*causal*)	ἐπεί
sing, I	ἄδω ἄσομαι ᾖσα ᾔσθην
sister	ἀδελφή -ῆς ἡ
sit, I ... down	καθίζω*, or middle καθίζομαι etc, καθέζομαι καθεδοῦμαι ἐκαθέσθην
I am seated, sitting	κάθημαι (*impf.*) ἐκαθήμην
six	ἕξ
six hundred	ἑξακόσιοι -αι -α
skilful	δεξιός -ά -όν
skill	τέχνη -ης ἡ
slander, I	διαβάλλω (see βάλλω*)
slaughter, I	σφάζω -ξω -ξα ἐσφάγην
slave	δοῦλος -ου ὁ, οἰκέτης -ου ὁ
sleep, I	καθεύδω*
slow	βραδύς -εῖα -ύ
small	μικρός -ά -όν
snake	δράκων -οντος ὁ
snow	χιών -όνος ἡ
it is snowing	νίφει (*aor.* ἔνιψε(ν))
so (*with adj.or adv.*)	οὕτω(ς)
(*with verbs*)	ἐς τοσοῦτο
= therefore	οὖν
so many	τοσοῦτοι τοσαῦται τοσαῦτα
so much	τοσοῦτος τοσαύτη τοσοῦτο
Socrates	Σωκράτης -ους ὁ
soldier	στρατιώτης -ου ὁ
solicitor	συνήγορος -ου ὁ
some ... others	οἱ μέν ... οἱ δέ
someone, something	τις, τι
son	υἱός -οῦ ὁ (*pl.* υἱεῖς)
son-in-law	γαμβρός -οῦ ὁ
soon	δι' ὀλίγου, οὐ διὰ πολλοῦ, τάχα
sorry, I am	*impers.* μεταμέλει (see Chapter 21)
soul	ψυχή -ῆς ἡ
Sparta	Σπάρτη -ης ἡ
Spartans	Λακεδαιμόνιοι -ων οἱ
speak, I	λέγω*, ἀγορεύω (usually only in present and imperfect)

speaker	ῥήτωρ -ορος ὁ
spear	λόγχη -ης ἡ, αἰχμή -ῆς ἡ
speed, at full	δρόμῳ
spend, I	ἀναλίσκω -αλώσω -ήλωσα -ηλώθην
splendid	μεγαλοπρεπής -ές
spot (= place)	χωρίον -ου τό
stade	στάδιον -ου (*pl.* στάδια or στάδιοι)
stand up, I	ἀνίσταμαι -στήσομαι ἀνέστην
state	πόλις -εως ἡ
stay, I	μένω*
steadfast	βέβαιος -α-ον
steal, I	κλέπτω*
still	ἔτι, ἔτι καὶ νῦν
stone	λίθος -ου ὁ
(*adj.*)	λίθινος -η -ον
I leave no stone	
unturned	οὐδὲν παραλείπω (see λείπω*)
stop, I	
= I detain	κατέχω (see ἔχω*)
= I put a stop to,	παύω -σω -σα -σθην
= I cease (from)	παύομαι -σομαι -σάμην (with genitive)
storm	χειμών -ῶνος ὁ
strange	δεινός -ή -όν
= foreign	βάρβαρος -ον
stranger	ξένος -ου ὁ
street	ὁδός -οῦ ἡ
stretch, I ... out	προτείνω -τενῶ προὔτεινα προὐτάθην
string	σχοινίον -ου τό
stroke, I	ψήχω -ξω -ξα -θην
strong	ἰσχυρός -ά -όν
Strophius	Στρόφιος -ου ὁ
student	μαθητής -οῦ ὁ
stupid	μῶρος -η -ον
stupidity	μωρία -ας ἡ
subdue, I	καταστρέφομαι -ψομαι -ψάμην
such, of such a kind	τοιοῦτος -αύτη -οῦτο, τοιόσδε -άδε -όνδε
suddenly	ἐξαίφνης
suffer, I	πάσχω*
suitable	ἐπιτήδειος -α -ον
suitor	μνηστήρ -ῆρος ὁ

summer	θέρος -ους τό
sun	ἥλιος -ου ὁ
at sunset	ἅμ᾽ ἡλίῳ καταδύντι
suppliant	ἱκέτης -ου ὁ
surprised, I am	θαυμάζω*
surrender, I (*trans.*)	παραδίδωμι (see δίδωμι*)
(*intrans.*)	ἐνδίδωμι
swan	κύκνος -ου ὁ
sweet	ἡδύς -εῖα -ύ, γλυκύς -εῖα -ύ
sword	ξίφος -ους τό
Syracusans	Συρακόσιοι -ων οἱ
table	τράπεζα -ης ἡ
take, I	αἱρέω*, λαμβάνω*
I am taken	passive of above verbs, or ἁλίσκομαι ἁλώσομαι ἑάλων
I take alive	ζωγρέω -ήσω -σα -ήθην
I take care that	εὐλαβέομαι -ήσομαι -ήθην (see Chapter 18)
I take in = deceive	ἀπατάω -ήσω -ησα -ήθην
I take off = lead off	ἀπάγω (see ἄγω*)
I take out	ἐξαιρέω (see αἱρέω*)
I take over	δέχομαι*, διαδέχομαι
talk, converse, I ... with	διαλέγομαι -ξομαι -ξάμην or -χθην (with dative)
tame	ἥμερος (-α) -ον
task	ἔργον -ου τό
taste, I	γεύομαι -σομαι -σάμην with genitive
tax	φόρος -ου ὁ
I pay my taxes	τοὺς φόρους ἀποδίδωμι(see δίδωμι*)
teach, I	διδάσκω*
teacher	διδάσκαλος -ου ὁ
temple	ἱερόν -οῦ τό
ten	δέκα
ten thousand	μύριοι -αι -α
terrible	δεινός -ή -όν
terrify, I	φοβέω -ήσω -ησα, ἐκπλήσσω -ξω -ξα ἐξεπλάγην
than	ἤ
thank, I	χάριν οἶδα*, χάριν ἔχω* with dative
that	ἐκεῖνος -η -ο

theatre	θέατρον -ου τό
Thebans	Θηβαῖοι -ων οἱ
Thebes	Θῆβαι -ῶν αἱ
Themistocles	Θεμιστοκλῆς -έους ὁ
then (= at that time)	τότε
(= next)	ἔπειτα
there	ἐκεῖ
from there	ἐκεῖθεν
to there, thither	ἐκεῖσε
therefore	οὖν (second word)
thief	κλέπτης -ου ὁ, ληστής -οῦ ὁ
think, I	νομίζω*, οἴομαι -ήσομαι ᾠήθην
this	οὗτος αὕτη τοῦτο, ὅδε ἥδε τόδε
thousand, a	χίλιοι -αι -α
threaten, I	ἀπειλέω -ήσω -ησα -ήθην
three	τρεῖς τρία
throng	ὄχλος -ου ὁ
throw, I	βάλλω*, ῥίπτω -ψω -ψα -φθην
I throw away	ἀποβάλλω
I throw into	εἰσβάλλω
thus, in this way	οὕτω(ς)
tie, I	δέω δήσω ἔδησα ἐδέθην (*pf. pass.* δέδεμαι)
timber	ξύλον -ου τό
time	χρόνος ου ὁ
for a long time	πολὺν/μακρὸν χρόνον
right time	καιρός -οῦ ὁ
today	τήμερον
tomorrow	αὔριον
towards	πρός with accusative
tower	πύργος -ου ὁ
train	παιδεύω -σω -σα πεπαίδευκα -θην
traitor	προδότης -ου ὁ
travel, I	πορεύομαι -σομαι -σάμην or -θην, ὁδοιπορέω -ήσω ὡδοιπόρησα
traveller	ὁδοιπόρος -ου ὁ
tree	δένδρον -ου τό
trial (in court)	κρίσις -εως ἡ
I put on trial	εἰς κρίσιν καθίστημι (see ἵστημι*)
trip abroad	ἀποδημία -ας ἡ
trireme	τριήρης -ους ἡ

Trojans	Τρῶες -ων οἱ
trooper	ἱππεύς -έως ὁ
troops	στρατιῶται -ῶν οἱ
trophy	τροπαῖον -ου τό
I set up a trophy	τροπαῖον ἵστημι*
trouble, I am in	ἐν ἀπορίᾳ εἰμί*
truce	σπονδαί -ῶν αἱ
true	ἀληθής -ές
truly	ἀληθῶς, ἀληθινῶς
trust	πιστεύω -σω -σα -θην
trusted, trustworthy	πιστός -ή -όν, ἀξιόπιστος -ον
truth	τὸ ἀληθές, (*quality*) ἀλήθεια -ας ἡ
truthful	πιστός -ή -όν
try, I	πειράομαι*
(in court)	κρίνω*
Tusculum	Τοῦσκλον -ου τό
twelve	δώδεκα
twentieth	εἰκοστός -ή -όν
twenty	εἴκοσι
twice	δίς
two	δύο δυοῖν
tyranny	τυραννίς -ίδος ἡ
ugly	αἰσχρός -ά -όν, δυσειδής -ές
Ulysses	Ὀδυσσεύς -έως ὁ
uncle	θεῖος -ου ὁ
unclear	ἄδηλος -ον
understand, I	συνίημι (see ἵημι*)
unexpected	ἀπροσδόκητος -ον
unexpectedly	ἐξ ἀπροσδοκήτου
unhappy	ταλαίπωρος -ον, δυσδαίμων -ον
I am unhappy, despondent	ἀθυμέω -ήσω -ησα
unharmed	ἀσφαλής -ές
unjust	ἄδικος -ον
unobserved by	use λανθάνω* (see Chapter 17)
unpalatable	ἀχάριστος -ον
untie, I	λύω -σω -σα -θην
unworthy	ἀναξίος -ον
up there, above (*adv.*)	ἄνω

uproar	θόρυβος -ου ὁ
urge, I	παραινέω -έσω παρήνεσα with dative
use, I	χράομαι*
useful	χρήσιμος -η -ον
vain, in	μάτην
vengeance, I take ... on	τιμωρέομαι -ήσομαι -ησάμην with accusative
verandah	πρόθυρα -ων τά
very much, very greatly	μάλιστα, σφόδρα
victory	νίκη -ης ἡ
I win a victory	νικάω -ήσω -ησα -ήθην
villa	οἰκία -ας ἡ
village	κώμη -ης ἡ
virtue	ἀρετή -ῆς ἡ
visit, I	ἔρχομαι* or προσέρχομαι πρός with accusative
voice	φωνή -ῆς ἡ
I use my voice, give utterance	φθέγγομαι φθέγξομαι ἐφθεγξάμην
vote for, I	ψηφίζομαι -ιοῦμαι -ισάμην
wait (for), I	μένω*, καταμένω
wake, I	ἐγείρω ἐγερῶ ἤγειρα ἠγέρθην
walk, I	βαδίζω -ιοῦμαι -ισα
wall	τεῖχος -ους τό
want, I	ἐθέλω*, βούλομαι*
war	πόλεμος -ου ὁ
warn, I	νουθετέω -ήσω -ησα -ήθην
waste, I (time)	τρίβω -ψω -ψα -φθην or ἐτρίβην, κατατρίβω etc.
water	ὕδωρ -ατος τό
way, manner	τρόπος -ου ὁ
we	ἡμεῖς
weak	ἀσθενής -ές
wealth	πλοῦτος -ου ὁ
weapons	ὅπλα -ων τά
wear, I	φορέω -ήσω -ησα -ήθην
weep, I	δακρύω -σω -σα
welcome, I	δέχομαι*
well	εὖ, καλῶς
I am well	καλῶς/εὖ ἔχω*

I am well disposed ... towards	εὖ φρονέω -ήσω -ησα (with dative)
when	ἐπεί
when ?	πότε ;
where (*rel.*)	οὗ, ὅπου
to where	οἷ, ὅποι
where ?	ποῦ ;
to where, whither ?	ποῖ ;
which (of two) ?	πότερος -α -ον ;
who, what ?	τίς τί ;
what kind (type) of ?	ποῖος -α -ον ;
who, which (*rel.*)	ὅς ἥ ὅ
whole	πᾶς πᾶσα πᾶν
why ?	διὰ τί ;
wide	εὐρύς -εῖα -ύ
width	εὖρος -ους τό
wife	γυνή -αικός ἡ
wild beast	θηρίον -ου τό
willing, I am	ἐθέλω*
willingly	ἑκών -οῦσα -όν
wind	ἄνεμος -ου ὁ
wine	οἶνος -ου ὁ
wing	πτερόν -οῦ τό
of an army	κέρας -ατος τό
on the right wing	ἐπὶ δεξιᾷ
on the left wing	ἐπ' ἀριστερᾷ
winter	χειμών -ῶνος ὁ
wisdom	σοφία -ας ἡ
wise	σοφός -ή -όν
wish, I	ἐθέλω*, βούλομαι*
with	μετά with genitive, σύν with dative, or use ἔχων or φέρων (see Chapter 17)
withdraw, I	ἀναχωρέω -ήσω -ησα
woman	γυνή -αικός ἡ
wonderfully	θαυμασίως (ὡς)
wood	ὕλη -ης ἡ
wooden	ξύλινος -η -ον
word	λόγος -ου ὁ
work	ἔργον -ου τό
written work	γράμματα -ων τά

work, I	ἐργάζομαι -άσομαι (*impf.* εἰργαζόμην) εἰργασάμην
world	οἰκουμένη -ης ἡ
worse	κακίων -ον, χείρων -ον
worsted, I am	ἡττάομαι -ηθήσομαι ἡττήθην
worth(y)	ἄξιος -α -ον with genitive
wound	τραυματίζω -ιῶ -ισα -ίσθην
wreck	ναυάγιον -ου τό
wretch, you (*voc.*)	ὦ κάκιστε
write, I	γράφω*
I write back	ἀντιγράφω (see γράφω*)
wrong, I do	ἀδικέω -ήσω -ησα -ήθην
Xenophon	Ξενοφῶν -ῶντος ὁ
Xerxes	Ξέρξης -ου ὁ
year	ἔτος -ους τό, ἐνιαυτός -οῦ ὁ
yesterday	χθές
young	νέος -α -ον
young man	νεανίας -ου ὁ
you	(*sing.*) σύ, (*pl.*) ὑμεῖς
your	(*sing.*) σός σή σόν, (*pl.*) ὑμέτερος -α -ον
Zenis	Ζῆνις -ιος ὁ
Zeus	Ζεύς Διός ὁ

Index

accents 122-7
accusative absolute 102
accusative case 2
adjectives 15-16
adverbs 17
agent 3, 103
aorist tense 19
αὐτός, use of 27-8
cases, use of 1-4
commands 55-7
comparative adjectives 16-17
conditional sentences 71-5
connection 38-40
dative case 4
definite article 6-9
deliberative questions 50
demonstratives 31-3
exhortations 56
fearing, verbs of 85-6
future participle
   expressing purpose 62
future tense 19
genitive absolute 23
genitive case 2-3
gerundives 102-3
grammar terms x-xviii
imperfect tense 19
impersonal verbs 100-1
indefinites 91-2
indirect commands 56-7
indirect questions 50-2
indirect statement 41-5
instrument 4

negatives 114-16
open conditions 71-3
optative, use of 113
participles 22-3, 79-82
perfect tense 20
personal pronouns 25-7
place 11-13
pluperfect tense 20
possessives 25-7
potential sentences 76
precaution, verbs of 86-7
prepositions 117-21
preventing, verbs of 87-8
principal parts 128-39
pronouns 25-8, 30-3
proper names 6
purpose clauses 61-3
relative clauses 35-7
result clauses 66-8
space 13-14
subjunctive, use of 113
subordinate clauses in indirect speech 57-8
superlative adjectives 16-17
temporal clauses 94-7
tenses 19-20
time 10-11
τίς/τις, use of 30-1
unreal conditions 73-4
vocative case 1-2
wishes 56